Designed by Ed Fredenburgh
Published June 2007 by
Camden–Abu Dis Friendship Association (CADFA)

Printed in Britain by Lightning Source

ISBN 978-0-9556136-0-9
EAN 9780955613609

© CADFA

THE FIRST SIX DAYS
الأيام الستة الأولى

الأيام الستة الأولى

THE FIRST SIX DAYS

Oral history of the Six-Day War in 1967: the beginning of the Israeli occupation of Jerusalem, the West Bank and Gaza Strip – remembered by people in Abu Dis and Camden

Edited by Nandita Dowson and Abdul Wahab Sabbah

CONTENTS

INTRODUCTION
    Nandita Dowson   ix

ABU DIS MEMORIES: 1
    Salah Ayyad   3
    Najah Ayyad   9
    Ali Ruman   17
    Ezzat Ruman   21
    Mohammed Ahmed Jaffal   23
    Hajeh Fatima Ahmed Jaffal   29
    Mohammed Abed Sabbah   33
    Salemeh Sabbah   37
    Sameha Hussein   39
    Hussein Ahmed Afaneh   41
    Omar Ahmed Afaneh   45
    Naimeh Othman Qureia   49
    Saleem Qureia   53
    Mohammed Mousa Jaffal   57
    Mousa Ismail Jaffal   61
    Sami Shehadeh Awad   65
    Abdullah Lafee Khilaf   67
    Mohmammed Shehadeh Mohsen   71
    Hajeh Im Mohammed   75

CONTEXT   79
    Salah Ayyad:
    1967 – the historical context   81
    Saleh Abu Hilal with Abdul Wahab Sabbah:
    Life in Abu Dis before and after 1967   87

MAPS
    Israel/Palestine after June 1967   92
    Abu Dis area, 1967   93
    Abu Dis area, 2007   93

CAMDEN MEMORIES   95
    Three memories from Camden   97
    Ruth Tenne, born in Israel   99

CADFA
    Camden Abu Dis Friendship Association   103

Introduction

The first six days

This year will see the 40th year of the Israeli Occupation of the West Bank and Gaza Strip*. As half the Palestinian population are children, and many are young, for most people in the West Bank the Occupation has been a fact for all of their lives and, for many of them, for most of their parents' lifetimes too.

As part of its work to promote human rights and respect for international humanitarian law, CADFA listens to the stories of Abu Dis people's lives, and puts some of these on our website, www.camdenabudis.org.

At this 40th year, we wanted to ask people who remembered the beginning of the Occupation in Abu Dis how the Occupation started, for them – and this book is the result.

Salah Ayyad, a member of the town council of Abu Dis, has written a historical context. Saleh Abu Hilal, a retired teacher has written about Abu Dis before and after 1967, together with Abdul Wahab Sabbah. In order to focus on people's memories themselves, though, this book begins with the stories of the first six days of Occupation as remembered by people from Abu Dis.

These stories of June 1967 are memories of panic and chaos, huge pressure on people to make massive decisions in minutes with only partial information. When we began it, we really didn't know what the stories would be like, but as it has gone on, we have been struck by a number of themes.

One is that of refugees. Abu Dis is next to Jerusalem and within sight of the hills of Jordan on the other side of the Dead Sea and the Jordan Valley. Built on limestone, there are lots of caves. Faced with the danger of war, people fled, to the caves, outside town, east to Jericho and on to Jordan. Then Israel tried to limit their return.

1967 was not the beginning of problems for the Palestinians. In 1948, with the first huge dispossession at the formation of the state of

NANDITA DOWSON

Israel, some of the first big wave of Palestinian refugees had come to Abu Dis, and two of them tell their 1967 stories here. But then in 1967, it seems that Abu Dis lost two thirds of its population in just a few days. And like the 1948 refugees, they have not been allowed to return.

A second theme that struck us is how much the worries people had at that time have continued to be the ones that dominate now.

The Occupation isn't a stable fact – it is restless, changing, constantly surrounding Palestinians with new rules, new "facts", new geography, making their attempt to live a normal life more and more impossible. Life has changed a good deal in the past 40 years - increasing restriction on Palestinians through passes, checkpoints, forbidden roads, land confiscation. From day to day, the Separation Wall is encroaching, bulldozers at work cutting trees for the next part, cranes building more illegal settlements and more buildings within them, army jeeps arriving in the remaining Palestinian areas at any time of day or night, establishing new checkpoints, lining citizens against the wall, raiding houses, taking youth prisoners to distant jails.

But right from the beginning of the Occupation, people have suffered from missing relations, divided families, problems with papers at checkpoints, problems travelling, dangerous army and random killings, attempts to make Palestinians leave Palestine. All of these things have continued and the pressures magnified as the years have gone on.

Relevant international law governing the Occupation has been constant in the past 40 years. The United Nations has called on Israel to leave the West Bank and Gaza. Refugees from war are supposed to be allowed home. The Geneva Conventions do not permit the confiscation of occupied land or building upon it or the movement of prisoners across international borders. And in 2004, an advisory opinion of the highest world court called on Israel to stop building the Separation Wall, remove what had been built, and compensate the Palestinians who had been damaged by it. The Court also called on other states in the world to stop Israel's violation of international law and ensure enforcement of the Fourth Geneva Convention. Israel has not complied with these international rules – that too has been constant.

While the governments of the world are deciding on their approach to this, one thing is changing, and that is that an increasing grassroots movement is growing in support of the human rights of Palestinian people. We began this project by talking to people in Camden about their memories of the Six Day War of 1967. Some people were very vague about it, mixing the memories of different wars and unclear what had happened. The other story remembered by a number of people, though, was Israel's version; Israel remembered as persecuted and brave - and the Palestinians, their rights and their suffering, invisible in the account.

There has been a real change of perception in Europe since then, however. While some time ago the dominant picture of the Middle East was of Israel's righteousness and perhaps of Palestinians as terrorists, this picture is now challenged. People brought up in ignorance of the history of the Middle East or with the stories of only one side are now asking to know the whole story.

The twinning movement is a growing part of this movement. With a focus on human rights and a respect for the equality of people, groups like CADFA are seeking to know and to tell the real human experience of the Palestinian people – and on the basis of what we find, people in Camden are joining people in Abu Dis in calling for their human rights under international law.

This book is dedicated to the children of Abu Dis and Camden, wanting the friendship between the two places to continue to grow, and the human rights of all people to be respected; and in the hope that when they are a little older and look back, the Occupation itself will be history.

Nandita Dowson
Camden Abu Dis Friendship Association
May 2007

Officially not occupied since Israeli withdrawal in 2005, the Gaza Strip is still imprisoned by Israel which also controls who enters it, flies planes low over it, brings its army in or bombs it at will; so Gaza is not free and therefore, really, the occupation is not over there yet.

The first six days

Abu Dis memories

Salah Ayyad

Salah Ayyad is now a local council member in Abu Dis.

On Monday 5th June 1967 I was sixteen years old and living in Abu Dis. At about 9 o'clock in the morning, the Arab radios started to talk about an Israeli aeroplane attack on Egypt, which means that officially the military operations had started between the Arab countries and Israel. This had been expected at any moment.

At that period there were no televisions in Abu Dis. Because of that, people started to gather around the radios to hear the different announcements from the Arab and the Israeli side about the war.

At about eleven o'clock in the morning, we heard heavy tank fire in Abu Dis. At that time, Abu Dis was a very important base for the Jordanian army, and from that location the Jordanian army started to shoot towards Israel, and at the same time Abu Dis was also attacked by the Israeli shell fire. Many Abu Dis people had not had the experience of war before, and everybody was nervous from the beginning. At the same time we all had the hope that we could get back our rights and this gave us a good feeling all the time we were under attack.

In the days before the war, people started to buy food, and because there were no shelters to use in the war, people started to clean the caves around their houses. The caves had been there in Abu Dis for hundreds of years – people used the caves to keep animals in and to store grain and animal food. Before the war, most of these caves were not in fit condition to have people inside them. Because of that, people prepared them. But they were big enough to hold everyone, as there are many caves in Abu Dis.

Also in 1967, there were no water pipes in Abu Dis, and people used to depend on the wells. These were full and ready at that time of the year. And because the period of the war was not long, the water was enough for people. Also because the use of water was limited – there were no electrical machines, so it was just for cooking and drinking. There was no shortage of water, either for the war or the period of curfew after the war.

At the beginning of the war, the Israelis destroyed the electrical supply and cut the telephone lines, although in Abu Dis there were not more than 6 or 7 telephones at that time. Also there was no clinic or first aid centre for Abu Dis – people could only go to Jerusalem for this service. Once the war began, Abu Dis became isolated from Jerusalem, which was its centre, and from the whole world, and there were no basic public services. In that period, there were about 6,000 residents in Abu Dis. There was no university then and no workers from the university. It is also worth mentioning that many Abu Dis people used to work in the Gulf States and in the east bank of the river (in Jordan). Because of that, many of them had left their families in Abu Dis, which caused a big movement of people during the war between Jordan and Palestine.

At nearly 12 o'clock on 5th June, while I was sitting outside my house together with some of my neighbours, a bomb fell on our neighbourhood, coming from the area where the international group used to be, on the green line. At that period, my father was in the East Bank, so I was responsible for my family. Directly everybody went to his family, and I gathered my family, and we came together – we were nearly 30 from the same neighbourhood – and entered a cave which we had prepared to be our shelter during the war. While we were collecting the children and the old women, many of the women started to shout and to cry, but we managed to calm them down and to organise things inside the cave. From inside that cave we followed the news from the war by gathering round our old radio.

On the first day of the war, there was heavy shooting, and the Israeli aeroplanes did not leave the area. The sound used to make the earth shake under our feet while we were inside that cave. I remember that I did not sleep that night and none of the others slept, and as for the children, they tried to sleep, but they kept waking because of the noise of the bombs and the aeroplanes.

On the first day, the food wasn't a problem – nobody even cared about food because everybody was nervous and scared about what was happening, but on the second day in the morning, we started to think about food, at least for the children. At that time, the economy in Abu Dis was self-sufficient – people depended on themselves - so every family used to have a piece of land around the house and used to grow vegetables and food on their land, and to raise chickens and goats, which was good for the people, and it was helpful for the people during the war.

In the neighbourhood I used to live in, there were many people who raised cows and sheep and used to sell milk and its products in Jerusalem. One of them was an old woman called Sheikha, who volunteered to prepare food for us from rice and milk. I went with her to her house and we brought one of her cows and some rice and she cooked behind the wall because she wanted to protect herself from the shooting and from the bullets. After that we carried the food to the cave and we fed everybody. This is how we used to make our food, from things which were available around us in the neighbourhood. We used to eat together, also. Of course there were no meat and vegetables which we usually used to eat, but under the circumstances which we were going through in that period, we did not think about food but were just eating to survive.

On the second day, the battles continued and the smoke covered all the area of Jerusalem, nearly half the way to Jericho. For myself, I did not manage to reach my sister who was in another cave, which was only a few hundred metres from our cave. She was living with her husband's family, because her husband was in the Jordanian army, and I tried many times to reach her, but I did not have luck because of the heavy shooting around. In general we managed to do our things in a good way and there was nothing that happened to any of the group that I was with in the cave. I remember entering the cave at sunset that day, tired and sleepy, so I lay down, and when I woke up, it was sunrise of the third day of the war.

It seems that people get used to a situation whether it's positive or negative, and you can say that they start to accept the atmosphere of war. Because of that, I woke up early and after we made food, I went directly to the nearby place, where my sister was living, and I brought her together with her two children and some things for them, and I brought them back to our cave to join the family. After that I went out to the west side of Abu Dis, to the Jordanian army place, and from there, it was clear that people were getting used to the war atmosphere and started to move between the different neighbourhoods in Abu Dis. They were bringing food for the Jordanian soldiers who had lost communication and were receiving nothing from their leadership, because the Israeli aeroplanes had destroyed the roads and the bridges. There I saw the houses which were on fire because of the napalm bombs and also I saw the olive trees also on fire, and they stayed burning for many days because they were big. On that day also I managed to find the names of the Abu Dis people who had been killed and injured over the past few days. On Wednesday, 7th June, we started to hear about the possibility of the Jordanian army withdrawing and the fall of Jerusalem and maybe all the West Bank.

When I returned back to our cave, I noticed that there were many people who used to be in our cave now outside, sitting behind a wall, and with them there were men, women and children – and I recognised them as having come from Jerusalem, specially from Al Thowri neighbourhood which was located directly on the east of Abu Dis. Most of them were children, suffering badly from hunger. We brought them milk and we made food for the adults and for the children.

These people who came from Jerusalem started to talk about how serious the situation was in Jerusalem, and about the killing and the humiliation of people which took place in their neighbourhood, and had forced them to leave. They advised us to find another safe place to hide, because if the Israelis captured us then they would kill us all, specially the young men. When we heard this, there was a serious feeling of fear among the people, and they started to discuss the idea of moving to another place outside the neighbourhood and out of Abu Dis, or even to cross the river to the East Bank, specially when we heard that there were many people from our family (Ayyad) who had already crossed the river and were now in Jordan.

There were many men from Abu Dis working outside, and people were afraid that if this occupation lasted for a long time, it would mean that the Israelis would close the borders, and these people would lose the opportunity to communicate with their families. This made many families leave to join their fathers or their husbands outside. Also, the refugees who passed through Abu Dis from Jerusalem made a terrible feeling of fear with all the stories that they had about the massacres that the Israelis were doing in Jerusalem, and led many people think of leaving to Jordan.

That night, my auntie came to our house with all her family, preparing to leave to Jordan. While she was there in our house on 8th June, my mother started to think of leaving with her. At that time, there were four of my brothers and sisters under eleven years old; also there were my older sister's two children with us. I could not imagine how these children could live in a refugee camp, waiting for humanitarian help from the United Nations, and also I could not imagine that we could live together with my mother in the government school, which is what the Jordanians had prepared for the refugees. Because of that, I had to face my mother, and we had an argument, and I announced that together with my brothers and sisters, I would never leave our house. I said, "I prefer to die here than to go and turn out to be a refugee."

After a long argument between me and my mother on that night and a lot of shouting, I convinced her to stay. My auntie, together with her family, left for Jordan together with her family. I did not meet her for many years, and that was after I travelled to Jordan with a permit, which the Israelis started to give to Palestinian people who wanted to go to Jordan.

On that day, at the time that the people were leaving to Jordan, my father arrived from Jordan. When we met together, he said that, in any circumstance, we must not think of leaving our house or our homeland. It was the same position which my uncle had, who had even refused to leave his house during the past days – he did not even go to a cave.

That decision from my uncle encouraged many people and it had a good effect on the families around, and because of that position, many families decided to stay and not to leave. More than that, my father and my uncle started to prepare coffee and food and water behind our house and in the street, and they used to give these to the people who passed near to our house and try to convince them not to leave and to return to their houses or to stay in our neighbourhood because there were many empty houses in the neighbourhood as their owners had already gone to Jordan. But the majority refused to listen to him, and people continued to go toward Jordan. Some of them used animals to carry their children, and their personal things. Other people from Abu Dis who left their houses asked us to take care of their houses and property and their animals.

After several days I started to go to their houses. When I entered some houses, I found there was heavy dust on the furniture and the animals and chickens had been left without food or water. Even the flowers had become dry because they did not have water. So I collected the animals and took them to our house, and I watered the flowers. And also I used to visit and check the houses till the owners returned.

There were many people who came back, crossing the river, during the coming weeks, and their return was usually during the night. In the morning each day we used to discover that there were many people who had returned.

During their journey back, many of them were captured by the Israelis and sent back to the east side of the river, and some of them were killed by the Israeli army. There were about 10 people killed, one of them was my best friend Mahmoud, who was also my cousin, and we used to be in the same class at school. Mahmoud went with his father to Jordan on the third day of the war. I tried to convince him not to go and to stay with me, but he refused and he joined his father and promised to return back to Abu Dis. But after one month, and while he was trying to cross the river together with his father, his sister and her children, the Israelis shot at them all and nobody heard about them and we did not even find their bodies.

On the last day of the war, and with the announcement of the ceasefire, nearly all the occupied territories were put under curfew, and people were without work. There were no schools because of the summer holiday and there was no electricity so we returned to the traditional gas lamps and each night we used to gather around the radio to hear the latest news about what was happening in our case, specially the discussions in the United Nations and the Security Council which took a decision asking Israel the occupying power to withdraw to its position before the war.

But what happened was that even with all these decisions and discussions, the Occupation is still here, and they have added many awful procedures as an occupying power. Now they arrest people, they confiscate lands… The Palestinians also had their uprising against the Occupation and they resist the Occupation – but despite all this, the Occupation is still there.

7

Najah Ibrahim Ayyad

From my memory – and what I've been told (I was seven years old).

Monday the 5th June 1967

Between ten and eleven o'clock before noon – it was the first day in the summer holiday – our mother was making lunch for us, Salah my brother was outside on our veranda, in front of the old family house. He was lying there holding my brother Khalid in one hand and in the other hand a transistor radio, listening to the news, and when they announced about the war, Salah stood up in a hurry. We were all around him – he held Khalid and the transistor and he shouted at my mother who was near the primus stove, cooking, because it was very noisy, and he told my mother "The war has started, turn off the fire and leave everything, let's go to the cave". He also started to call our relatives, specially the young men to go inside the caves before the children and women, and check that everything was OK, there were no insects or snakes or any dangerous thing inside the cave.

They took a fire torch and they entered the cave and they started to put it inside the gaps and the small holes inside the cave in order to check there was nothing dangerous in there. They cleaned the cave and they asked the women and the children to enter. We took our necessary things and we entered while I heard people around me say "The war has started and nobody knows how long it will go on". All the people in our neighbourhood entered that cave which couldn't even hold any attack. The war started and we started to hear the sounds of the planes and the sound of shooting from everywhere.

The cave was not ready, and there was nobody ready for the war. This cave had been there since many years. It has a very small door. It was surrounded by rocks and the ground was bare earth, full of holes. It was not even good for the human beings to use it. The women started to cry because they were afraid about the youth and the children and the young girls and in particular about people who were away outside Palestine. They did not know whether they would meet them again. My mother was crying, firstly because my father and my brother Saleh were not there – my father finished his military service in the Jordanian army, retired and he was ready to return back, and my brother Saleh was a student at the Military School in al-Zarka. Also my mother was afraid about Saleh because she had him after she lost two children and there was just one girl older than him. Because of that my mother was very protective of him, unable to believe that he was actually still alive. All of us children were crying with her. The children were sitting there inside the cave looking at their mothers. They did not exactly know what was happening, while the adults were gathering round the transistor radio, listening to the announcements and analysing what they heard from the news. Some of them were happy with the results and some of them did not believe what they were hearing, and some were hopeful for the future and some were afraid of tomorrow.

Throughout the war period, there were Jordanian military tanks passing through Wad al-Jheer and we used to see them taking position in the middle of the valley – they put their weapons and their tanks near Abu Dis Boys' School and they also prepared a military first aid centre in Abu Dis Girls' School (where the youth centre is now). There were also soldiers near the Arab Jordanian Institute (near where the Al Quds university is now). In that period I liked to hear the national songs which used to be broadcast by the Sowt al-Arab Radio (from Egypt), such as "We will return back by the force of arms."

On the day before the war, in the morning, a truck full of tomatoes came from Jericho, and the driver told the women "You have to buy because the war will come any time". He wanted to return back to Jericho before it started. The women bought some and he asked them to take the rest free because he wanted to return to Jericho, but I don't think that he returned before the war started. People just prepared in this way for the war – they bought food."

I don't know exactly how much time passed before the war ended. It was very short. My brother Salah asked the people in the cave to bring all the extra food that they had to send to the Jordanian army in the valley. People told Salah that he was joking – how could he go out in these circumstances? But Salah, who was very young – he was not even 17 – used to have a brave heart and a respected voice, took the water and the food and went to give it to the soldiers.

In the meantime, the shooting was very heavy, and my mother was very sad because Salah did not return back. Everybody was waiting for him to return, but my mother now had two sons and her husband out of the cave and in danger. When Salah returned back, he told everybody that the Jordanian army soldiers did not have anything to eat and they did not have any food or military supplies, so at that time my mother cheered up and she said that Salah's life was not more precious than the soldiers' lives or our homeland, so she also went out to the caves around us and she started to ask people to give any extra food to her to send with Salah to the Jordanian soldiers, and Salah set off to take it. And I remember that our cousin, Ali Shakkah went with him.

I don't know exactly how many days passed, but we all heard a voice calling us from outside, with our names. Everybody heard it, and when my mother went out, she discovered that my father had returned. Everybody inside the cave was happy, because it was a good sign for the other families which had their fathers or their sons outside. My father said "Do not go out, I will come inside because it is very dangerous outside," and he greeted us and hugged my uncle, Abu Yassin, who used to be the main politician inside the cave, who gave analysis about what was happening outside, and the women used to enjoy his analysis. Also my uncle Raghib, who used to have a gun, was there with his wife, but all his children were away.

When my father reached my mother and greeted her, she shouted at him "Where is Saleh?" He said " Don't be afraid. It was a risk to bring him back with me but I left him in a safe place in Jordan – he is OK. When she started to cry, he said that Saleh would come tomorrow after they would have the victory – that was the hope. After we asked him how he had come from Jordan under these circumstances, and what news he had about the road, he told us, "I left Jordan one day before the war, and I walked all the way, and I hid when I felt that there was danger – What do you think? It is war."

My father refused to sleep inside the cave because the house was near the cave, so he went to the house. This had a good effect on the people around us, it cheered them up and encouraged them to return to their houses at least to check what had happened to the houses and to bring anything they needed. The women cooked to feed the children inside the cave.

I remember that they announced on the radio that Jerusalem had fallen. I realised it was on the 5th June. Jerusalem, flower of cities, had fallen. The heritage of Omar al-Khatab and Salah al-Din had fallen. The conspiracy had been accomplished. The al-Aqsa Mosque and the church had fallen.

The men and the women started to cry together. Nobody believed what they heard, but then the people who lived in the West of Jerusalem started to escape towards us and to assure us that this had happened and Jerusalem had fallen.

Abu Dis was the road to Jordan. People were very afraid to go on the main streets because the Israeli aeroplanes used to bomb the roads and to kill the people there. Because of that, people preferred to go between the houses, in a place called Dahareh Marj al-Sulatan, which is now called Harat al-Halabiyeh. So they used to go by foot to the countryside on their way to Jordan, whole families, children without any shoes on, and in their pyjamas came from Silwan and al-Thowri, two areas of Jerusalem. I remember that there was a family from al-Thowri, brothers with their women and children, they came to al-Thahara and my mother asked them to enter, and she prepared a place for them to sleep. The children were crying and their feet were bloody, and they came at night. My mother lit a gas light and she started to help the children by taking thorns from their legs. When my father asked them why they had left their houses, they said that the bombs were near to their houses and they had left everything, they had even left food that was cooking still on the fire, and they had not had an opportunity to change their clothes.

My father used to ask everybody not to leave our homeland but the memory of the massacres in Deir Yassin was still in their minds. My father got some mattresses and brought them out on the street and made some coffee and put pots of water on the street for anyone to drink so anyone who passed our neighbourhood could eat and drink and have a rest. Some people used to hold their children on donkeys. There was a woman who passed with her children on a donkey, and she cried out in a very loud voice and said "We have lost our homeland." My father said, "We will lose our homeland if we leave it," but she refused to stop and she continued. And it was the first day of our defeat.

The streets were full of people. Groups used to come and others used to leave. The news used to come – things you could believe and things you couldn't believe. The propaganda reached everybody – things that happened and things that didn't happen. Women used to cook for the people who came from Jerusalem, and here I remember the truck with the tomatoes, and one of our relatives, Uncle Mousa, who used to have a cow with plenty of milk, as he did not have the opportunity to sell the milk, so he donated the milk for the people. About the cooking, besides the bread, there were two main dishes, one was rice with tomatoes and one was rice with milk, which they used to put on one big tray and share together.

One day we heard my father shouting and threatening, and when we asked him why, he said that people had come from outside Abu Dis and said that the Jews entering the houses had killed the young men and raped the girls and they advised us to run away from our neighbourhood. This made our relatives very afraid, and they said to my father that we must run away and leave this place, because they were convinced by that story. Most of them had young girls like my sister whose husband was in the Jordanian army and we did not know anything about him, and she had two children. Until then, my mother had been very busy thinking of Saleh, but things had changed and his sisters were now in danger...

But my father stopped everybody. He said "If anybody tries to leave this area, I will kill him myself, and if it is true and the Israelis are raping the girls, and if anything happens to one of your girls, I will marry her to one of my sons." Because of that, none of us left our neighbourhood; we stayed put and we are still there till now.

Near Abu Dis Boys' School, the Israeli army came and they had a camp there. That was the first time we saw the Israelis. When they reached that place, the people who lived around the school left their houses and they came to us – Most of them were our relatives. My father told them not to leave their houses, not to go out of Abu Dis, till we saw what would happen. He went to their houses and called to the people who were still there to stay in their houses and not to leave. At that point the policy for the Israeli army was not even to talk to people and to let them go if they wanted to leave their houses because the important thing for the Israelis was to make people leave their houses and even to leave Palestine. They used to shoot after them after they left their houses because they didn't want them to come back again. The people used to ask their girls to put on very old clothes, clothes for old women, because they didn't want the soldiers to notice that they had young girls and to rape them. Also people set out to Jordan in groups, and many groups got lost, and nobody knows what happened to them, till now.

Things started to be clear and we found that many of the stories which we had heard were lies and not true. Before that, the people started to search in the places where the Jordanian army and the fighters used to hide, and they found bodies of people who had been killed. They buried them in Jabal al-Mukabar. I heard there was a cave called al-Bashir cave: the people found many bodies of Jordanian soldiers inside it.

Also there was a story during the war about some Jewish women who held a white flag. So the Jordanian army thought they were surrendering – but when they came near to the women, they discovered it was a trap from the Israeli army, who arrested the Jordanian soldiers and took them to Ras al-Amoud and there they killed them all.

The war period was very short, and some eye witnesses said that the soldiers from the Jordanian army used to pass through Abu Dis. They said they were running away from al-Latron area, because that area had fallen in the hands of the Israelis. The people from al-Bakaa, al-Latron and al-Thowri ran away from their houses in terror believing the propaganda that the Israelis used to pass to them, about killing people and raping women. And they didn't even want to stay in Abu Dis because they were very scared about their children and their women. Many of them were on their way to Jordan. The Israeli aeroplanes used to bomb and kill them. The result was that the people in Abu Dis did not know about what had happened to the people who left to Jordan, and the same for the people who reached Jordan – they did not know exactly what had happened to the people left behind in Abu Dis.

Because of that, people in Abu Dis started to think about going to Jordan to search for their relatives and to tell people about the news in Abu Dis. They used to go secretly in the night and to cross the river at a place called al-Mukabar. They used to spend some time in Jordan and return back with news and letters from the people there to their relatives.

One of them was a man called Jameel (Abu Ahmed) who used to bring letters, and the women in our neighbourhood used to wait for him at my Aunt Khameeseh's house – They used to wait for him each day and wait for the letters.

My brother Saleh was still in Jordan, so my mother asked my father to go and bring him. That night, my father woke up at 3 o'clock in the morning and he told us that he wanted to go and cross the river to Jordan. When he arrived in Jordan and met Saleh, my auntie's husband was also there and wanted to return to Palestine with her five sons and husband.

But on the next day, my auntie's husband went out before my father and my brother Saleh. It was early in the morning. When my father arrived on the east side of the river, he heard gunfire on the other side of the river, so he hid on the Jordanian side and returned back to Jordan. When the people in Jordan asked him about my auntie's family, he said they were now in Abu Dis. But in Abu Dis, nobody arrived and there was no news about them.

I don't know exactly how much time passed with no news of them, but my father later heard that the gunfire had been on them. When one of them (my cousin's husband) turned up, nearly naked, in Abu Dis, he told everybody that he had lost his whole family – his wife and five children, together with his father-in-law, and he was the only survivor. He said that the last thing he heard was gunfire and his sons shouting – he didn't know exactly where they went – he returned back in the morning to the same place and he did not find anything, even their bodies. Until now nobody knows anything about them – after 39 years.

My father and my brother, who were supposed to come with him, did not show up, so my mother did not believe that they were still alive – she thought they had died with everybody, and she did not believe that they were alive until they returned back after 3 days, together with another family from Abu Dis.

People were very sad in Abu Dis because a whole family had been killed, together with another young man from Abu Dis, Ahmed Eriqat. At that time many other people were missing and nobody knew if they were alive. My mother was very busy with my auntie all the time. She used to leave us from the morning to the afternoon.

The Jews started to appear on the streets in East Jerusalem, and people were really afraid, specially in Jerusalem. My father also used to go to Jordan to convince the people to return because there was nothing to be afraid of, and because the people in Jordan were living in schools and refugee camps, and the winter was coming and it is very hard to stay inside a tent or a camp in winter. Many of them returned by crossing the river at night, and in many stories the women returned before the men and the girls, to protect their houses, and then the rest of the family returned.

There were some people who went out early in the morning from Abu Dis, and they used to collect letters from people from here and there. They used to put them in a cement sack together with some old clothes – they floated them on the water so they would reach the other side. The idea was that if the Israelis caught it they would think it was just old clothes – and the letters inside would go in the water and get destroyed. In the evening when they returned, they used to bring with them some letters from the people on the other side.

Some time after the war, after some nights, a military operation took place in Abu Dis, A young man who used to live in Abu Dis shot at an Israeli military jeep that was passing Wad al-Jheer area. They shot him in his leg. When he returned back to his home, they followed the trail of his blood, so the Israelis decided to punish Abu Dis by making a curfew. They asked all the people in Abu Dis to go out of their houses and to go to Abu Dis Boys' School. After that, a huge military force came to Abu Dis and they started to search the houses.

At that time, my father was in Jordan. They came to our house and they forced us all to stand by the wall. As you know, my brothers Saleh and Salah were 20 and 16 years old, but Salah was taller than Saleh and he looked older than Saleh, When the soldiers asked them and Salah said that he was younger than Saleh - Salah and Saleh were standing near the wall with their hands in the air – one of the soldiers started to beat Salah on his back with his gun. My mother started to cry while my brother Khaled who was 3 years old was shaking. She tried to protect her sons but she couldn't so she started to blame my father because he refused to allow us all to go to Jordan.

Everything was over and the Israelis destroyed the house of the man who had fired the shot, and arrested him. They also destroyed a small house near his house, which belonged to an old man who used to live alone. There was no one to take him out of his house so he died under his house.

There was another story. All the people in our neighbourhood remember it. It was when the Israeli soldiers came and they took a young man called Hussan Ayyad from his house and they accused him of hiding a gun under the rocks of the dry stone wall. They asked Hussan to destroy his own dry stone wall, rock by rock, and one of the soldiers hit him in his face and others started to kick him. I will not forget his face when the blood was running. He destroyed the wall and they did not find anything, but anyway they took him to their jeep and they started to beat him. All the people of the neighbourhood saw that happen. After that time, his mother, who was sick at the time, did not see him before her death, because he decided to leave Palestine. He went to Spain and got married and never returned to Abu Dis.

The Arab and Jordanian soldiers used to pass through Abu Dis. They were hungry and thirsty and women in Abu Dis used to give them water and food. Once a Jordanian solder came to our water well and he drank water. My mother asked him "When was the last time you ate?" He told her "Three days ago, and I haven't found anyone to feed me." At that moment an Israeli aeroplane passed above us and that soldier wanted to shoot at it. My mother shouted at him and told him to keep his bullets "If you shoot at them, they will bomb us and destroy us all – So we will feed you and after you finish your food you can go anywhere else and you can fight." She cooked him rice and milk and gave them to him to eat, and he ate and left.

When the Israeli army searched our house and beat my brother, my mother decided to go to Jordan. But my father had told us, before he left for Jordan, that we should not go, or run away; he was convincing the others not to leave, so how could his family go to Jordan? So my brother Salah told my mother and all of us "If you want to go then you can go alone; I will not leave my house and I will stay with my brothers here". And now we are all thanking God that Salah took that decision, because if we had left at that period then we would never have come back here again.

The war ended and we returned to our ordinary life. My mother used to have a permit to go to Jordan and also put my little brothers on that permit to take them with her. When she arrived in Jordan alone, she used to go to al-Abdali area in Amman and ask if there was any child who had lost his family and wanted to return back to Palestine; she would bring them back with her under the name of her son Khalid.

After the war, the Arab army left Palestine and they left their weapons and ammunition exactly where they were. The Israelis saw them and left them near the houses and the people, just to remind us that we were weak and that the Israeli army had beaten the Arab army. They used to capture anybody who came near these weapons and punish them. This ammunition brought very bad things for Abu Dis and harmed many people in the village. Once a group of children, the oldest one was 12 years old, went down to the valley, and they collected some bombs and played with them. One of the bombs exploded and it killed one of the children and injured three. One of them lost his eyes. Abu Dis still remembers that story, when people heard an explosion and went down to the valley and found that child's pieces and collected them and buried him. Because of that, Abu Dis people started to collect the ammunition by themselves and to get rid of it away from their houses and the village.

Of the other stories from the war, I remember when al-Aqsa Mosque was burned by an Israeli terrorist. He set fire to the mosque and all the people from around Jerusalem tried to protect it. At that time the Israelis said that man was crazy, and some of the Arab leaders believed them. We have many many good people in the Arab countries and Israel has many crazy people, but with our good people we lost our country and our homeland, and with their crazy people they built a country of nuclear weapons.

15

Ali Ruman

Ali came originally from a village called Souba which is 12 km west of Jerusalem. His family left the village in 1948, during the first war, and lived as refugees in Abu Dis. Till 1967, they used to live inside a cave in Abu Dis. He was about 22 at the time of the war.

This is the area on the south of Abu Dis, full of caves. Many people came here in a hurry when they left Abu Dis

Our memories stopped in 1948 when the Israelis forced us to leave our village and we lived for nearly 20 years as refugees, waiting and hoping that one day we could return back to our beautiful village, Souba, where we left our house and our trees and our land. When I heard about the war (in 1967), on the Monday, the first thing that came to my mind was "Here has come the time that we will return back to our homeland and liberate Palestine." In that period we had this hope and we were very happy, although it was war and we knew that we would suffer during it.

On the first day, exactly at 11 o'clock, we heard that the war had started, and from my house I saw Israeli rockets hit a Jordanian camp that used to be behind our house. So we stayed in our cave (which used to be our house) till Wednesday when two Jordanian soldiers came to our cave and told us, "The war is over and the Arab armies are beaten, and if you want to stay alive you have to leave Abu Dis."

I started to think about emigration, which would be the second time in my family's life. I took my father, my wife, my son and my three brothers, and I went east. In Abu Dis there was a square called al-Khanafseh Square, where people usually used to meet. We went to that square, hoping we could find Abu Dis people and hoping we could find a solution for our situation – maybe the people in Abu Dis would have another solution, better than going outside. But when we arrived at that square, we found it empty, there was nobody there, so I decided to continue my way to Jericho.

When we reached the main road near al-Mrussuss, I saw waves of people, nearly 3,000 people on the road, walking east, while the Israeli aeroplanes were in the sky, watching. Also there was an Israeli aeroplane that was hit and fell down, and we saw the pilot on fire.

When we arrived at Jericho, I entered an empty house together with my family. At that time also the Israeli army invaded Jericho from the north. We spent two hours before the Israeli army entered the house and asked me to take my family, hold a white flag and go to the mosque – the Saleh Abdu mosque in Jericho. I took my father's kaffiyeh, which was white, and I divided it into two; I held one and my old father held one, and we walked in the street. There were many other people holding white flags and going to the mosque.

When I entered the mosque, there were thousands of people there, maybe more than 2,000 people, children, women, men all together. We spent one week inside that mosque. After three days, on Friday, Jamal Abdul Nasser who was the leader of Egypt at that period, announced on the radio that the Arab countries had been beaten in this war, and he also announced his resignation. At that time we were inside the mosque, and there was an Israeli tank outside the mosque, and hundreds of soldiers. I remember that at that time we thought that this was our end, and the Israelis would now kill us all inside that mosque.

At that period I started to remember also that I had heard a month before the war that the Jordanians received a shipment with a huge number of fireworks and I wonder what exactly the Jordanians wanted to do with this number of fireworks. Also I remember that Asim al-Mo'ayetah who used to be the leader of the Jordanian army in Jerusalem started to move his furniture, his family and his money to Jordan a month before the war. This can explain the results of the war, even in advance. But for myself, I was more positive than anybody, because we considered that this war must return us back to our homeland.

On the same day, which was Friday, two civilian Israelis came to the door of the mosque, and asked if there was anybody inside who could speak English or Hebrew. I told them I could speak English (I was a teacher). My family, specially my father and my wife, were very scared about me, and my father asked me not to go outside. When I went out, I discovered that these two men were from the Israeli television, and they asked me who was inside. I told them there were more than 2,000 people, most of them women and children. They asked me whether we had food inside. I told him no, and nobody was thinking about that until now because we did not know what would happen to us. Then he asked me to join them in a pick-up car and, with the soldiers, they started to open the shops in Jericho and to ask me to take anything from the shops to the car; so I collected wheat, sugar, tea and anything else I found inside the shops, and we returned to the mosque.

At that time, all Jericho was under curfew like the rest of the West Bank, and we were not allowed to go out. I remember that there was a man hiding in a house on the other side of the street – his name was Kamel Far'on, and his brothers were with us in the mosque. On Saturday morning, he tried to cross the street to join his family. The Israeli soldiers around the mosque shot him and he was on the street bleeding till he died after more than 6 hours.

On Saturday in the afternoon, some soldiers and a general from the Israeli army entered the mosque for the first time, and they gave us two choices. If anybody wanted to go to Jordan, there were buses outside and we could take them. But if anyone wanted to back to his home town, they had to stay and wait. Nearly half of the people inside the mosque went out to go to Jordan but as for me and my family, we preferred to return back to our cave in Abu Dis rather than be refugees one more time. So we decided together to stay inside the mosque.

One thing that I remember while we were in the mosque, my three-year-old son dropped hot tea on his body and I did not know what to do. I asked the soldiers outside to let me take my son to Jericho hospital and they allowed me – but I did not find anybody inside the hospital. So I started to use different medicines and put things on his body.

Another thing that I remember was that inside the mosque there were guns and ammunition from some Jordanian soldiers who used to be in there. We decided to get rid of this because we didn't want the Israelis to see it. Together with some of the people inside, we hid them inside our clothes and threw them outside without letting the Israelis notice.

On Wednesday, they came to us again, and they said if we wanted to return to our villages then we could go. But if we wanted to travel, we weren't allowed to stay on the main road after 5 in the afternoon because there was a curfew, and if they captured any of us then we would be taken to Jordan.

So we decided to go on foot from the mosque to Abu Dis, with the temperature very high, which totally damaged our legs. First we lost our shoes – they were destroyed by the walking and the temperature, and then we had to walk barefoot. When we arrived at al-Khan al-Ahmar, we met an Eged bus (an Israeli bus); we asked the driver to take us to Abu Dis because it was late and we didn't want to be caught by the soldiers or they would take us to the Bridge to go to Jordan. When we arrived in Azariyeh on that bus, it was curfew, and we spent that night in Azariyeh sleeping on the ground under the trees. The next day, Thursday, after 9 o'clock in the morning, when they stopped the curfew, we went back to Abu Dis to our cave.

About things that I remember, first I remember the Jordanian soldiers who got rid of their uniform. That was because the Israeli aeroplanes used to shoot them from the sky even if they were among the people. Another thing from my memory was what happened to Atta Erikat, who was the bus driver who was killed in al-Salt while he was driving a group of people from Abu Dis to Jordan. In al-Salt, the bus was attacked by an aeroplane, and while the driver was trying to escape from the bus together with the other people, a Jordanian military vehicle hit him and killed him.

I also remember another bus that left Abu Dis on Thursday, the fourth day of the war, and while it was on the road to Jericho, in al-Khan al-Ahmar, the bus hit a wall and all the people inside the bus had to continue to Jericho by foot.

Another story I remember well is about a man called Thabit Salah - he used to be a teacher in that period - and when the people ran away from Azariyeh on the first and second days of the war, he did not manage to go out because he was ill at that point; so he gave his four children to other people to send them to Jordan, because he wanted to protect them. And he spent four years after the war asking and searching for his four sons, until he found them and got them back via the Red Cross.

About Ahmed Mattar, he helped people to return back across the Israeli bridge after the war. He helped more than two or three thousand Abu Dis and Azariyeh people return to their houses.

Ezzat Ruman

Ezzat was also a refugee who originally came from Souba to Abu Dis in 1948. He remembers that at that period he was about 19 or 20. He used to be a volunteer in the Jordanian army, and when he heard about the war, he went directly to Abu Dis Boys' School, which is the place that his commander had told him to go to if there was ever an emergency situation.

I left my family with the rest of the people from Souba, and I went directly to do my duty in the army as a volunteer. For more than five months before the war, we used to train on different weapons to be ready to fight. But when we arrived at Abu Dis Boys' School – there were nearly a hundred of us – our leader told us that he was still waiting for a decision from his leaders about whether to fight and whether to give us weapons. When our leader went to the Jerusalem government, Jordanian of course, they refused to give us weapons to fight.

Because of that I left the school, and I went after my family to Jericho. When I arrived at Jericho, there was fighting inside the town and the bullets came from everywhere; so I continued my way to the river. There I spent nearly 15 days helping people at al-Mukabar to cross the river in both directions. We used to make plastic and cardboard into boats and put people inside it and send them to the other side, specially the children who couldn't swim.

I remember that when I returned back to Abu Dis after 15 days, there was a curfew, and the Israeli soldiers were invading houses and searching for weapons and for fighters.

One story that I will never forget is about a man in Abu Dis called Khader Abu Hilal. When the Israeli soldiers invaded his house, they stole his watch. That man was very brave and he went directly to the commander of the Israeli army on Jabal Abu Kamel (the same place where they have the military camp now) and he complained to them that the Israeli soldiers had stolen his watch. There the commander asked him if he could recognise the soldier who stole his watch, and he said "Yes". When the soldier came, he told the commander which soldier it was, and he returned his watch.

This picture was taken in the al-Mrussuss area by an Israeli soldier. It shows Abu Dis refugees returning from Jericho to Abu Dis

Mohammed Ahmed Jaffal

In 1967, I used to own a café. I heard about the outbreak of war from the Sowt al-Arab Radio (the Egyptian radio station). I was about 40 – I had been a soldier in the Jordanian army, and I knew exactly where the Jordanian army places were, specially the one near Anatta, which included tanks. There was also a camp in the old Abu Dis Girls' School which was near my café.

When the war started, the soldiers in that camp asked me to help them to put a telephone cable between their camp and the camp at Jabal Abu Kamil, where the Israeli military camp is now. So I took the cable and went towards the camp in Jabal Abu Kamil with two Jordanian soldiers. After I finished this job, I returned to my café where I met the leader of a special Jordanian force, and together we appointed the targets we wanted to shoot in West Jerusalem. It was ten o'clock on Monday morning.

When we started to see the Israeli air force in the sky, the Jordanian officer asked me to shut down the café and to go home. That night I spent with my family in my house.

On the second day, the bombing reached Azariyeh: an Israeli aeroplane shot and burned one of the houses in Azariyeh. Because of that I decided to go to a cave near my house, and there together in that cave there were thirty people from different families.

On Tuesday in the middle of the day, one of my relatives returned from Jordan, and he said that the Iraqi army were in an area in Jordan called al-Mufraq, and they were now on their way to Jerusalem. At the same time I saw Jordanian tanks coming from the west and they stopped near my café – I saw them from the house. I went to them straight away. I noticed that one of the tanks had more soldiers than it could take. When I asked the officer on that tank about the situation, he told me that two of the tanks had been hit, and because of that, they were taking the soldiers from those tanks with them, and they were going towards the east. From his own tank radio, he called all the Jordanian force to move east.

After that, I decided that Abu Dis was not safe for me or for my family to say in, so I returned back to the cave to find that there were more and more people coming to that cave. I told everybody that since the Iraqi army was coming, there would be shooting between the Iraqi army and the Israeli army, and the battle place would be Abu Dis. So I decided to leave Abu Dis, along with all the people who were in that cave.

We went out. We were nearly 80 people. We reached an area called Arqoub al-Khail (where the university is now). On Wednesday morning, we met three Jordanian soldiers – they were trying to find out about any Jordanian force around. They told me that the Jordanian soldiers in Jabal al-Mukabar had been killed, and that they were the only survivors.

So I showed them the road to al-Khan al-Ahmar, and, as a man with military experience, I told everybody that the war was ended and the Arab army was beaten. I asked my sister to return back to my house and to bring me my gun and all the bullets that I had, and to close the doors of the house. And to be sure that the house was secure. One of my brothers decided to take his family and go to Jordan.

When my brother left for Jordan, I took my family and some food that we had, and we returned to the old neighbourhood of Abu Dis. We met some people from Abu Dis – most of them were soldiers in the Jordanian army. We decided together that it wasn't acceptable to leave the village, and we had to resist.

We started to see aeroplanes in the sky and we thought they were Algerian, till they started to shoot directly at the houses in the west side of Abu Dis. The people had decided to resist, but the first thing we had to do was to put our families in safe places and to return. I took my family and all the women and children and sent them to the place called Abu Suwan. I took them to a cave – there were fifty families there – and I returned back to Abu Dis.

By that time I had not slept for two days, and I was exhausted. So I decided to sit down and try to sleep for a while. I was less than a kilometre from Abu Dis.

Before I even fell asleep, I met some people. They were holding their furniture on a donkey, and they said they were going to Jordan. They told me that Abu Dis was now empty, there was nobody in the village, and it was very dangerous to return to the village, because the Israeli army was actually in the middle of Abu Dis.

Since my six daughters were then alone with their mother, it was not easy for me to make a decision to leave them on their own. I returned to Abu Suwan where I had left my family, and there we decided that all of us would go to Jordan – there was no hope in staying while the Jordanian army and the Arab armies had left us alone.

I took my family and my sister's family and we went directly to the main street. I stopped a car there with a Lebanese plate and I asked the driver to take some of my daughters with him, together with an old woman and my niece. Also there was a little disabled girl – we put them all together in that car and asked the driver to send them to a safe place.

After that we managed to stop a truck that was holding nearly 100 people. My brother joined him to go to Jericho, to get fuel and return to us. He took two more of my daughters with him – so now I had two daughters with the Lebanese driver, two with my brother in the truck, and two with me and my wife.

After nearly two hours, the truck returned to us, and we got inside the truck with the rest of the people who were waiting. While we were travelling to Jericho, nearly at al-Khan al-Ahmar, I saw my two daughters and my niece by the side of the road. I asked the driver to stop, and I asked them to come inside the truck.

When we arrived at Jericho, nearly at the market, I found many people from Abu Dis. Among them there were my two other daughters. The truck continued to the mosque in Jericho, and we found that the Israelis had already entered Jericho, so right away we asked the driver to continue to Jordan.

On our way, we found two Jordanian soldiers and they asked to join us on the truck, but we asked them to get rid of their uniform, and especially their hats and their weapons, because we were afraid that aeroplanes might shoot at the truck.

We reached the place near the river called al-Maghtuss, and there were two trucks, ours and another one, with 350 people between them.

On Thursday night at nearly 10 o'clock, we arrived in Amman. There we met a police car which asked us to turn off the lights of the truck. They told us to go to a square in the middle of Amman and sleep there instead of in the mosque, as there were many people inside the mosque. We followed them, and they gave us blankets and food, and they put us in a school where we spent the night.

In the morning, I asked the truck driver if he could take me and my family to Madaba where my brother Ismail was. We left early in the morning and when I arrived in Madaba and asked about my brother, I was told that he had gone to Ma'in to the mountains, because he wanted to see what was happening in the West Bank from the mountains there. So we waited for them. They returned in the middle of the day, and I left my family with them and returned to Amman again to bring my sister and her family to his house. When I came back to Madaba with my sister, there were nearly 65 people in his house – he couldn't hold us all – so we spent that night some of us in his house and some in a cave near his house.

On Friday morning, I asked the governor of Madaba, whom I knew, to open the church for us – I had served with him in the army and I knew him. So they opened the church and they brought us food, but a friend of mine from Jordan came and asked me and my family and my relatives to join him and sleep in his house. We spent two nights in his house, but after that I decided to take my family and my sister's family and to go to al-Zarka. We rented two rooms in al-Zarka and we spent 29 days, twelve people in two rooms.

My sister decided that she would return to Abu Dis, so I took her with her three children and I went to al-Mukabar, which is on the Jordanian river, where people used to cross the river.

When we arrived there it was early in the morning. I helped them to cross to the west side of the river and I waited for them till they had crossed the borders and got away from the west bank of the river. I returned back to al-Zarka to my family. The next day my nephew came back to me and told me that everything was OK in Abu Dis and we could return.

The same night, we heard an announcement on the Jordanian radio, asking us, all the refugees, to go to the Wahdat refugee camp. I went there and I found somebody from the Red Cross. They asked me to fill a special application with the names of my family members and a special request to return back to my homeland.

Even at that time, I felt that this wasn't serious. Even the Red Cross employees told me that this would not help us, but they wanted to register us all for their records.

The return

On the 23rd July, after nearly 2 months, I heard that there were people from West Jerusalem who had come and occupied my house, so I wanted to go back to Abu Dis. I discussed this with my brothers and one of them decided to stay in Jordan. I rented a car and I went to the river area. There were drivers calling for people to join them – did anyone want to go to Nablus, to Jerusalem, to Jenin? We were fourteen people on a pick-up – my family and my brother-in-law Saleh's family. When I asked the drivers there, they advised me to go either very early in the morning or after eight o'clock in the evening; and they told me that the safest area was called Kareemeh, which is 50 km north of al-Karameh. First I asked one of the drivers to take me by myself so we could be sure that the area was safe before I brought my family.

So I went with the driver, and I discovered that this area was for people travelling to the north, to Nablus, Jenin and Toubas. It was secure and we could cross from there.

So I returned to my family and we took the pick-up in the afternoon. The drivers there told us there were two different groups who worked with people to help them to cross the river, one in the night at 10, and the other one at 4 o'clock in the morning. There was a room on the west side of the river where people could stay before they went on to Toubas. Each one had to pay 2 Jordanian dinars to the guide who would help them cross the river and for the bus which was supposed to wait on the other side of the river.

I told them that I wanted to cross at 10 at night, and we entered the water. It was very shallow and easy for us to walk. When we arrived on the other side of the river, we discovered that there were many people waiting for the bus to come and take them to Toubas, which was 2 km away from the river.

I met a group of people – there was a teacher in Dar al-Aytam School, and two men from Maythaloun near Jenin. My daughters asked if they could go and have a bath in the river so I asked the guide if we could rest for a while. It was in a wide place, full of crops, specially tomatoes. The two men from Maythaloun refused to stay with us; they said they knew the place and they wanted to continue.

Five minutes after they left us, we heard very heavy shooting. It was very close to us, so I asked everybody to lie down on the ground and not to move. Actually there was an Israeli military tank half a kilometre away from us and the shooting went on for nearly 15 minutes. The guide told us that there was a military camp and that this tank would go there. He recommended that none of us should move until we were certain that the tank was gone. So we lay on the ground for nearly an hour and a half and I told all the people with me, "Even if you want to go to the bathroom, you have to do it where you are, do not move."

At nearly 12 o'clock, the tank moved, and our guide said that it was going towards the camp, so since we were the first people who crossed the river, we decided to move to our west. But after less than 10 minutes the tank returned back and again they started to shoot.

I hid my family near a stone wall and this time we stayed till 4 o'clock in the morning, lying on the ground. There were 21 people including my family hiding behind this wall. At 4 o'clock in the morning we left, after the guide told us that the tank was gone, and when we passed a small hill we found the road, and on the road we found the bodies of the two men from Maythaloun, dead, and their blood was all over the road. It seemed that after the soldiers had shot them, they had cut the bodies in pieces.

I was holding two of my daughters and I ran away from that side because I didn't want my daughters to see this sight. We walked in the road till we found a taxi; I waved to the taxi and I begged the driver to take us with him. We were sixteen people in that taxi. The driver told me that each hour there was an Israeli tank that moved from the camp to the river. He said if they stopped us, it was important to say that we were originally from Toubas and we had been on our land, and we were going home now.

It was easy – we managed to pass near the camp, and we reached Toubas at 7 o'clock in the morning. I asked him to take me to one of my friends in Toubas, but when we arrived at my friend's house, his neighbours told me that he had left for Jordan and he had not come back. Of course, there was no reason for me to stay in Toubas, so I went down to the main street to find a taxi for my family.

I asked one driver to take me to Abu Dis, but he said that it wasn't possible to go to Jerusalem without a permit and he advised me, if I wanted to go to Abu Dis, to go first to Jericho. So that is what happened. I went with him, together with my family, back to Jericho. When we arrived near al-Fara'ah refugee camp, he stopped the taxi and he wanted me to make a story that we were originally from Talluzah, and we were going to Jericho to one of our friends there. On our way, an Israeli soldier stopped the taxi and asked the driver if he could take him with us to Jericho. When my daughters were very afraid and started to cry, the driver told him "The girls here are scared and I can't take you with us".

So we reached Jericho, went to the bus station and we went by bus to Abu Dis.

When I got to my house, there were three families living there, while my sister was living in a cave near my house. I went directly to my house, asking to have it back, but they threatened me that they would tell the Israeli camp, so I had to spend ten days in a cave. I went to the Mukhtar in Abu Dis, who advised me to go to Jericho Municipality, and to ask them to give me a letter to prove that I was in Jericho during the war and I had not been out of the West Bank. I managed to get that letter, went with the Mukhtar to Jerusalem, and we met the military governor who was a Jew from Yemen. I told him my story, and that there were three families in my house now, and he said that Abu Dis was under the control of Bethlehem, not Jerusalem, and that I had to go to Bethlehem.

So I returned to Abu Dis. Instead of going to Bethlehem, I went directly to the people in my house, and I threatened them that if they did not leave my house, we would attack them all, and we would throw them out of the house. I had a long discussion with them, and in the end, they asked me to bring them a truck to put their furniture on, and they asked me to pay for the truck, and this is what happened. I brought a truck and helped them to pack and in the end I had my house back.

Hajeh Fatema Ahmed Jaffal

Hajeh Fatema started by talking about her situation before the war. Her husband had died in 1956, leaving her with 3 children, the oldest one aged 10 years. She used to live in a small asbestos room in the Ras neighbourhood in Abu Dis. Then she talked about the 1967 war.

On Thursday 5th June at nearly 11 o'clock. I heard from the loudspeaker on the mosque that the war had started. At that time I was preparing food for my children. After I heard about the war, I took my two sons and went to a cave which is near to my house. Many families from that neighbourhood also arrived in that cave, tens of them came, fifty, sixty people were there. That night, many of the people from that cave went out of the village.

Next morning, my oldest brother came to me and asked me to bring my children and any necessary things for them, food, clothes etc and to go with him to the east hills of Abu Dis because the Israeli soldiers were starting to bomb the houses and the roads in Abu Dis. I started to collect the necessary things. I put out some food for my chickens and goats and I sent my cow to one of my neighbours who preferred to stay in the village and not to leave.

After that, I went to my brother's house and met all my brothers and sisters and their families there – the number was 64 – all of them came. When the dark came, we all went out to an area called Jowar al-Coton. People used to use that area for grazing for animals. Everybody went to a cave there and we spent Wednesday night in that cave.

During that night, a pregnant woman came there and she went into labour. The women there tried to help her to give birth. Meanwhile the men tried to sneak to the village to see their houses and their properties. Some of them managed to get to their houses and to bring some necessary things for their families from their houses.

In the morning, Mohammed Jaffal, who is my oldest brother, went to the village, and he met one of the Jordanian army officers, who told him that the Jordanian army had been told by their officers to withdraw to the east side of the river. Mohammed Jaffal returned back to us in the cave and told us that we needed to go to the main road between Jericho and Jerusalem, because we had to go to Jordan.

When we arrived at the area called al-Mrussuss (which is now the area of Maale Adumim settlement), the Jordanian army started to pass us, leaving their weapons behind them. This made many of the people in Abu Dis and al-Mrussuss area leave towards the east. Many of the young men went to the main road, and they started to stop vehicles and commercial cars and buses Mohammed Jaffal managed to stop a car – it was an Opal with a Lebanese licence. The driver said that he was going to Amman so Mohammed Jaffal asked him if he could take some of the children with him. That is what happened – three of his girls and my daughter Salemah Sabbah, who was 13 years old at that period.

My brother Yussuf managed to stop a truck which used to take building materials to Jordan from the West Bank, and he put the women and the children in that truck, and there was no space for the men to go with them, so most of them went east on foot.

It looked like Armageddon – everybody was rushing for his life and with what he could hold for his children, and to go away from that area – people waited to find any safe area to protect themselves from what was coming. My sister Naameh – her son was 7 days old – she threw him on the back of the truck where everybody put their clothes because she could not hold him as well as my other brother who was 2 years old.

After that the truck moved to Jericho. On our way to Jericho we saw many dead bodies on the sides of the road, especially in that area called al-Khan al-Ahmar, because that area used to be an operation area for the Israeli planes which were bombing everything that moved on the ground. Suddenly I saw the four girls that went with that Opal and the driver, including my daughter Salemah, on the ground, waiting for help near the area of the Khan. (It turned out that driver was an Israeli officer and his job was to give signals to the Israeli planes and to collect information about the Jordanian army.)

The girls jumped on the truck and we continued on our way to the middle of Jericho. There was gunfire everywhere and the Israelis reached Jericho at that time. There was resistance from the city. Because of that, the truck continued directly to the King Hussein Bridge and we managed to pass it before the Israelis destroyed it.

We went on to Amman and they went to the Hussein Mosque – that area was the place where all the refugees who left Palestine gathered – and when I left the truck, I discovered that my eldest son, Mohammed, was not there.

(his story follows)

31

Mohammed Abed Sabbah

The oldest son of Hajeh Fatima Ahmed Jaffal, Mohammed was about 21 years old at the time of the war.

I used to work on the Mount of Olives, and when I heard heavy gunfire in Jerusalem on Monday, I returned back direct to Abu Dis by foot. I remember that at that time, I started to think about the victory that the Arab countries could make against the Zionists and that we could return back to Haifa and Jaffa and Acre after the Arab countries had liberated Palestine. I was disappointed when I saw the Israeli aeroplanes starting to move in the sky of East Jerusalem and around it.

On that day, I saw that some soldiers from the Jordanian army had occupied the British representative's building on Jabal al-Mukabar. The Jordanians asked the internationals to leave the place, but because of the heavy fire from the Israeli aeroplanes and because there was not enough ammunition with the Jordanian army, they started to call over loudspeakers to the people from Sawahreh and Abu Dis, to ask for weapons and bullets. Many of the young men from Abu Dis went to Jabal al-Mukabar holding weapons for the Jordanian army, but the heavy Israeli bombing of the valley between Abu Dis and al-Mukabar meant they did not manage to get there. So the Israeli bulldozers smashed the Jordanian soldiers under them after they finished their ammunition.

I left my family at al-Mrussuss area after I did not manage to find a place in their truck. I went walking on foot to Jericho and at al-Khan al-Ahmar area, I met a family from Abu Dis. Among them they had a disabled child and the family were seriously discussing leaving her behind as no one could carry her any further, so I took her on my shoulders and carried her to Jericho.

When I arrived in Jericho, there was shooting everywhere. The bullets entered all the houses and I could not find any safe place to stay and I continued, running, to the river Jordan. When I reached it, I found hundreds of people who had gathered there, wanting to cross the river. It was not easy for anyone to cross the Jordan as the water was very,

very fast and it was dangerous for people who couldn't swim. Many people were killed crossing the river.

I managed to cross – I could swim – and I managed to reach Amman and I met my mother who had been waiting for him for the last day. Sixty four of us went to Madaba and we spent three days in one room altogether. On the fourth day, I took my mother and brother and sister and went to al-Zarka. We spent twenty days there before my mother decided to return to Abu Dis.

Our way back to Abu Dis was not less dangerous than our departure. Our family arrived on the east side of the river and we waited there till the night. The water was deep enough to reach our heads. I was the only one that could swim. I carried my brother and my sister first and then I went back for my mother.

On the west side of the river, we saw more than 20 dead bodies of women and children lying on the ground. The Israeli soldiers used to fire randomly during the night and the bulldozers buried the bodies all together on the following day.

After we returned back to Abu Dis, within 3 days, my mother asked me to return to Jordan with a message to my uncles, but this time I crossed the bridge legally. She sent me to ask my uncles to return from Jordan because they had left their houses and when she returned to Abu Dis she discovered that the Israeli authority had given her big brother Mohammed's house to a Palestinian family who had left their house in West Jerusalem.

Because of that, her brother Mohammed returned back, and he suffered many days just to convince those people to leave his house, and all the time they used to threaten him with the Israeli army. In the end, he managed to have his house back. In that period, many Abu Dis people lost their houses specially on the west side of Abu Dis, and the Israeli excuse was that when the Israeli soldiers entered the houses during the war, they were empty.

Out of the 64 people from the family who left that night to Jordan, only 23 managed to return back, and the rest are still now in Jordan.

35

Salemeh Sabbah

Salemeh was seven years old at the time of the war.

Salemeh is showing the cave that she and her family hid in during the war

We heard about the war and I went with my family for three days to stay in one of Abu Dis' caves. When we heard that the enemy had occupied the West Bank and the rest of Palestine, it was early in the morning, about 2.30 in the morning on Wednesday. On that morning, my mother prepared bread for us and everybody started to get ready to go outside to Jordan.

We walked for a long distance whiles the Israeli aeroplanes were bombing different places and the main road to Jericho. When we reached the main street, we saw a car with Lebanese number plates so my uncle stopped the car and asked the driver to take just the little girls with him. There were six daughters of my uncle and me with my little brother, together with the son of my auntie who was 8 days old at that time.

We got inside the car. Of course none of us knew the driver or where he came from. It was very crowded inside. There was also another old woman. We sat on top of each other till we arrived in the area of al-Khan al-Ahmar. There were military things happening there – there were soldiers and aeroplanes were throwing bombs on that area.

When that driver stopped, he told us to get out of the car, and he left us alone, without our families. I was the oldest. I was seven years old. The baby which we had, the son of my auntie, was crying, so I found a woman who was feeding her child and I asked her to feed Ta'seer (the baby). The woman asked me about his mother and I said "I don't know where she is".

We stayed there from 9 in the morning till 4 in the afternoon, when my uncle came in a big truck holding nearly eighty people. They were very surprised when they saw us. They picked us up. While we were on our way to Jordan, I saw many dead bodies at the sides of the road. We saw many children who couldn't even walk.

Sameha Hussein

Sameha Hussain's family house in Abu Dis built in April 1967, She and her family left this house in June and they were not able to return to it again

At the beginning of the war, I was in my house, alone with my five-day-old son, Sabbah, when I started to hear heavy shooting. When I felt the danger, I ran away. I went down to a cave near my house in such a hurry that I even forgot my child – I was not yet used to having a child. I realised what had happened and went back right away to take the child.

That night, my husband and his brother and family also spent the night in the cave, and in the morning we went down first to al-Mrussus to spend a day there, and then we continued on to Jericho.

In Jericho, we went to the mosque, and found it very crowded inside, so we separated into two groups: I was with my little son and my husband, and the other family stayed in the mosque with the people. I went with my husband to the bushes in the Jordan valley, where he asked me to stay while he went out to find food and water for us all.

After several hours, my husband had not returned. I started to hear shooting around me, and decided to leave that area, to try to return to the centre of Jericho.

So I spent that night alone with the little baby, and in the morning I managed to reach the mosque. When I arrived in the mosque, my brother's wife was in the mosque, also alone, not knowing where my sons or daughters had gone. My husband was in Jordan. My sister-in-law eventually found my children in the mosque, and they joined a family to return to Abu Dis, walking.

At that time, my husband was looking for me, and some people from Abu Dis told him that I might have gone to Jordan with my brothers, so he went directly to Jordan, and for seven days we did not know exactly what had happened to each other. I arrived in Abu Dis; he went to Jordan. My husband sent for me to join him in al-Zarka in Jordan, and since then our family has not returned to Abu Dis.

Hussein Ahmed Afaneh

I used to work in Jerusalem building what is now the National Hotel. I was in my thirties at the time of the war.

On 5th June 1967, I heard about the war earlier than everybody. They started from Egypt when they announced that all the Egyptian aeroplanes were destroyed while they were on the ground, so I understood that the war was already finished.

I went out from Salah al-Din street and I tried to find some transport to go to Abu Dis from Jerusalem – It was nearly 11 in the morning – but I did not find any transport to Abu Dis. Together with a friend of mine from Silwan, we walked all the way to Ras al-Amoud. When we reached Bab al-Amoud (Damascus Gate), I saw between 10 and 12 Jordanian soldiers. They started to shoot in the air and to take their positions around the Wall (there was a wall between East and West Jerusalem) Near al-Musrara the Jordanian soldiers started to shoot at the wall that divided Jerusalem, so I ran away together with my friend to Ras al-Amoud, then my friend went to Silwan and I continued to Abu Dis.

When I reached my home in Abu Dis, I found that my wife had already fed the children and collected all the valuable things from the house. We used to hide our money in our bed frame at home. We took the money and our children and went direct to my father's family house which is in the old neighbourhood in Abu Dis. There we found everybody in a cave near the house. There were my brothers, my sisters and my mother, and the wife of my brother who used to be in the Jordanian army, and her children, all together in one cave.

On that day and during the night, I held my transistor, hoping there would be some changes in the war. I heard the announcements by the Arab armies, specially from Cairo, and I also heard the bombing from the Jordanian army, who were on the other side of the Wad al-Jheer valley, shooting towards the west.

I remember that in the morning I went with my sister to my mother's house to bring some things – that is not far away from the cave. Near the door of the house there was an aeroplane, and it threw a container of explosives on to the main street in Abu Dis. I put my sister on the ground and I had to protect her with my body.

At that point I discovered it was over and the Israelis were already there, so I decided to take the children and the women and to send them out of Abu Dis to the east, but I myself did not go with them. My two brothers took the women and the children and they left, and I spent two days in the same cave, alone, guarding the houses and watching the results of the war.

On Wednesday, I saw a troop of Jordanian soldiers and military vehicles crossing Wad al-Jheer (the main road in the valley) and they were going east. Seven men from different families went down and stopped them. There were nearly 500 soldiers, all Jordanian. We said, "Why are you leaving us alone?" They said they were making a new plan – they wanted to go down and go round to Bethlehem to fight the Israelis. But of course it wasn't true: the Jordanian army was preparing to withdraw from the West Bank. It was the first sign that the war was officially ended and the Jordanian army beaten and they were running away.

On that day, together with some friends, I went directly to the main street in Abu Dis, the place where our families used to meet together, near the old mosque in Abu Dis. There I met five people from different families in Abu Dis, together with many Gypsies who had run away from Jerusalem, specially West Jerusalem, to hide in Abu Dis. Now the Jordanian army had left the city, they wanted to return to Jerusalem. We walked with them, and when we reached the main street between Jerusalem and Azariyeh, we call it Ras Kubsah, we found an Israeli checkpoint, and they divided us. They took the Gypsies because they knew they didn't have any documents, and they allowed them to pass to Jerusalem. For us, they asked us for our passports. It was very clear that we were villagers because we wore kuffiyeh, our special clothes. When they saw our passports, they let us go to Jerusalem. Of course there was no transport so we walked. When we reached Bab al-Isbat (Lion Gate), we saw the Israelis celebrating their victory – they were dancing. And when we reached the place which was supposed to be the border – the wall (between East and West Jerusalem), we discovered the Israelis had destroyed it and they had cleaned it all up as if it had never been there.

We passed the borders and we reached Jaffa Street, which was full of life, the market was open, and I saw many Palestinian children selling small things to the Israelis as if everything was quiet and there had not been a war. We did not notice that even one glass in any window in any building had been broken. It means that all the shells that the Jordanian army used to shoot from Abu Dis did nothing – nothing at all was destroyed.

When we returned back to Abu Dis, we had a meeting together, each family from Abu Dis sent a representative, and we had a decision to count everybody in Abu Dis so we knew who was there and who had left.

On Friday, my family returned, but I discovered that one of my brothers had left to Jordan together with his family, and also there were two sons of one of my sisters who was in Saudi Arabia at that period, and they wanted to go to Jordan to join their family. On the 12th day after the beginning of the war, I decided to go to Jerusalem to send my nephews to their mother in Jordan because we had been told that there were buses sending people free to Jordan from Jerusalem. When I arrived at Bab al-Amoud (Damascus Gate), I saw ten tables with people around them and about 10 Eged buses (Israeli) and people around the tables asked me to write the names of the children and send them on the bus. I put them on the bus together with my brother Omar, who was 16 years old – he was the oldest of them – and after that I returned to Abu Dis to have the meeting with the family committee.

And after the count we discovered that in Abu Dis there were 992 people. There had been 6,000 people before.

During the next 3 months many people returned. This used to be announced on the loudspeakers on the mosque, in order to cheer the people in Abu Dis so they knew that people were coming back.

One story about a woman in Abu Dis, who is a widow. During the three months, she went nearly 50 times to Jordan. She used to work as a post woman, collecting letters from Abu Dis and to take money from people who wanted to send their letters to Jordan (5 Jordanian dinars for each letter) and then she returned back with letters and news from the other side. How she crossed the river … there was a man called Ibrahim from Sawahreh. He had a small plastic boat and he used to cross the river carrying passengers, taking 10 JD from each person. It was still a dangerous thing to do. People could cross the bridge going east but the Israelis didn't let them come back west.

My brother, whose name is Hussan, who left Abu Dis to Jordan, sent me a letter with that widow, asking me to collect all his furniture and everything inside his house and send him everything to Jordan. So we collected all of Hussan's furniture and we sent everything by truck to the bridge.

On about the 15th day after the beginning of the war, there was a call from the mosque that there was a convent where they were distributing flour, and they gave each person one kilo, so they had something at least to eat.

Another story, about my brother's family, who had gone out of Abu Dis to find a safe place to stay. The reason they returned was they asked the Bedouin for some bread. One of the Bedouin told another, "Give bread to the refugees." My brother's family didn't want to be refugees, they were on their own land, and because of that they went back to their houses. They decided they would rather die in their houses than be called refugees.

When they returned to their house, Israeli soldiers came to the house, and one of the soldiers came to their well, and he threw some rubbish in it. My sister shouted at him – "How can you do this? This is the place we drink from." But he pretended he did not understand.

Also I remember the incident that took place in the valley when some children from Abu Dis played with some explosives and there was a huge explosion. I was the first one who arrived there. When I saw one of the children cut to pieces, I threw up. I didn't know what to do, I started to shout. As I remember from that explosion, there were two children killed from the Ayyad family, and one lost his eyes. After that we decided to collect these explosives and the Israeli army came and took them.

The Jordanian soldiers left Palestine for Jordan – one of them was my brother of course. On the bridge, the Jordanian army gave them their salary for three months in advance, and told them to go to their houses and stay in their houses. My main concern was my brother Yousef, as he was in the army and we did not hear about him. We thought that he had got killed. He used to be in Nablus in that period. But one night, after two months, a friend from the Abu Hilal family came to us in the night and he said that Yousef was in their house and afraid to return back home – He was planning to hide for a while and he would return when everything was quiet.

About people who got killed in 1967 – I remember Ismael Albow and Ahmed Ereqat and the family of Qadri Albow, his wife and four children, Dawood Jaffal, Mahmoud Jaffal, and another man also called Mahmoud Jaffal, who used to be a soldier and was killed in the war, Rizaq Abu Hilal.

Omar Ahmed Afaneh

I was 16 years old at that time. I heard about the war from the radio. Before the war, I used to be active against Jordanian rule in Palestine, in the West Bank, and one time I was caught by the Jordanians and beaten because I raised the Palestinian flag in a demonstration in Jerusalem. So I had my own experience with the Jordanians. Because of that, I did not have high expectations about the results of the war.

On the first day of the war, I joined my family and more than 50 people and we spent the first night in a cave near our house.

On the second day we all went outside Abu Dis and I spent a night with my family in a cave the countryside, and returned to Abu Dis on Thursday in the afternoon. When I returned, I saw Israeli aeroplanes bombing a camp of the Jordanian army in al-Zayam. That night, two Jordanian soldiers came to me and they asked me to give them some blankets and food, so I gave them the food and went with them to see the soldiers who were near Abu Dis Boys' School. There, the soldiers asked us if we could take some ammunition and weapons to the army on Jabal al-Mukabar, so I brought a donkey and I put a box of ammunition on it and I went towards the west, to the valley between Abu Dis and Jabal al-Mukabar. Unfortunately I did not manage to reach the hill because of the heavy shooting from the Israeli side into the valley.

On Wednesday, the Israelis started to shoot at Abu Dis houses, and there were many houses hit by the Israeli bombs. Among them was the house of Mohammed Khalid Eriqat and the house of Abu Adel Shabeh, who was killed inside his house when an Israeli napalm bomb hit his house. Also the house of Mohammed Qassim. Also the house of Ahmed Mousa Hamed. There was a bomb also that hit Abu Dis Boys' School, together with the house of Atta Ali, and destroyed them. That day, in the afternoon, Wednesday, I went down to Wad al-Jheer valley, to find two men from Abu Dis from the Jaffal family, with two donkeys – they had put their furniture on the donkeys, and they told me that they were going to Jordan. Together with a friend of mine, I took a small bag of my clothes and I joined them.

When we reached the area near al-Mukabar, on the river, it was very dark and they told us to sleep till the morning and we would cross in the morning. But when I woke up, I discovered that the two men had just crossed the river and left us behind – so we decided to return again to Abu Dis.

When we approached Jericho, we saw an Israeli checkpoint stopping the people and all the buses and vehicles which were returning from the city and the area near the river, and they were asking people and checking even their clothes. If they were wet showing they had crossed the river, then they were sending them back to Jordan. I hid with my friend and we managed to pass around the checkpoint. But after we reached al-Khan al-Ahmar, an Israeli jeep caught us and they gathered us together with other people who were caught there and they put us inside 3 buses together and drove us back to Jericho.

The buses stopped in a police station near Jericho which used to belong to the Jordanian police, and a soldier came inside the bus and asked if there was anyone who spoke Hebrew. One sheikh replied that he could speak Hebrew, and asked them just to give us some water to drink. But they refused. We stayed on the bus till 11 in the evening. After that the buses headed towards the Allenby Bridge to take us to Jordan.

But when the bus arrived at the bridge, I don't know what happened, because the bus decided to take us back to al-Khan al-Ahmar again. When we arrived there, they just dropped us and asked us to go back to our villages.

When I arrived at my house it was Friday morning. I discovered that my family had returned to Abu Dis so my brother took me directly to Bab al-Amoud (Damascus Gate) in Jerusalem, to send my nephews to Jordan. So I went with my nephews to Jordan, across the bridge, but under fake names, not under our own names – because at Bab al-Amoud they asked everyone to sign their name and say that we were going to Jordan without any pressure and that we were not coming back.

So I gave them a false name, and I went with my nephews to Jordan. After we crossed the two bridges to al-Shouneh, just the other side of the bridge. I managed to find a car and we had a lift to Amman, where I met my other brother and I gave him the children. I spent four days in Jordan before I headed back to al-Shouneh. There were three of us, me and two friends of mine, and people told us that if we wanted to cross the river, we had to cross at night, we couldn't cross in the daylight. From al-Shouneh, we walked nearly 15 km in the night, before we reached the east side of the river. There, while we were walking, a man with a gun came to us and asked us to follow him. He took us to a small room he had and he told us, "If you want to cross the river, you have to hide here till we have the signal from the other side that it is OK to cross."

At nearly 11 o'clock, the signal came to us, and we swam together, and we crossed the river. There were also nearly 15 other people who crossed with us, and we walked as a group, trying to avoid the Israeli camps and the Israeli snipers. When we reached an area called al-Alami Project, near Jericho, we heard a gunshot, and directly found we were inside an Israeli military camp. Me and my two friends from Abu Dis, we hid inside a huge tank of water, and we saw the Israeli soldiers capture all the people who were with us. The gunshot had been at one of them, they killed him, he died. They took the others all back to the river.

When they left, we had the opportunity to get out and continue on our way.

When we reached Azariyeh, we were told that there was an Israeli checkpoint near Ras Kubsah which is in between Abu Dis and Azariyeh, so me and my friend Adel decided to cross the valley between Abu Dis and Azariyeh and avoid the checkpoint. But our friend, whose name was Khalil Hassan Eriqat, decided to continue to the checkpoint because the road was easier. They captured him and returned him to Jordan, and I did not meet him again for ten years, till I went to visit Jordan. He walked all the way from Jordan and they captured him here, near his house, and took him back.

After a week in Abu Dis under a curfew, I decided to return back to Jordan. I went to the bridge, walking, and this time I crossed the bridge. I spent fifteen days there and then I returned back again. When we returned back, I crossed the river with nearly two hundred people. It was the night before Dawood Jaffal got killed.

The first time I saw the Israeli soldiers, it was Thursday, the fourth day of the war, in the afternoon. I remember the curfew stayed in Abu Dis for more than a month after the war. I remember that once the Israeli army came to our house, asking for water. I also remember the first military operation in Abu Dis against the Israeli army – that night I was together with two of my cousins, sitting at the front door of our house, when we started to hear the guns shooting in the Wad al-Jheer valley. While we were sitting there an Israeli jeep came to us, after the shooting, and they asked us what we were doing, and they asked if they could have tea with us. I refused to stay and I went directly to my house, to my room, but what happened to my cousins Ibrahim and Dawood Afaneh, was awful, because the soldiers drank the tea, and then they arrested them and beat and tortured them, asking them questions about who shot at the Israeli soldiers, to see if they had any information. As a result of that my cousin Ibrahim went to Jordan, and he did not return back till 1993.

I remember the children who played with the bombs and one of them was killed and one lost his eyes. When we heard the explosion and I went down to the valley, I saw a friend of mine called Mohammed Ayyad, running in circles, going crazy, with many people chasing him trying to calm him down but no one could, and I saw Abd al-Kareem Ayyad lying on the ground, bleeding from his face. Abd al-Kareem is now a doctor in the university, but he lost his eyes then.

I did not realise that another person was killed till the people started to collect his pieces.

Hajeh Naimeh Othman Qureia

Hajeh Naimeh was about 38 when the war started.

Rizq Dawood Abu Hilal was killed in Jericho by the Israeli soldiers while trying to find a way to take his family back to Abu Dis. His family took his body back to Abu Dis after the war

On the 5th June 1967, when the war started, I was living in al-Ras neighbourhood together with my eight children. The youngest one was 3 years old, and my oldest daughter was seventeen.

When I heard about the war, I was alone because my husband was outside, so I took my children and I went directly to a cave that is near our house, because there was no other place that is safer than this cave for me and for my children. But the thing that I missed doing was to dress my children in good clothes, because I thought that we would return home soon. I didn't take any food or any clothes.

We spent hours in the cave before some of our neighbours came to us and asked us to join them in another cave. It was not easy for me to make this decision and to take the children alone without asking my husband, specially as five of my children were under ten years old. After the Israeli air force started to bomb buildings in Abu Dis and Azariyeh, all the people in the cave decided to leave.

I remember our neighbour who refused to leave the house because her husband was not there – she did not want to go to the cave without his knowledge. She spent the first night of the war inside her house. She said that the walls of her house were shaking with each bomb that fell in the area. I convinced her to leave with me, and after several days of the war, the house fell down.

I left al-Ras neighbourhood with my family without having the opportunity to go into my house again.

We reached al-Mrussuss, an area east of Abu Dis. There were many people gathered there from Abu Dis. I spent two days in al-Mrussuss in a cave and I saw the Israeli aeroplanes throwing bombs all the way along the main street to Jericho. They were bombing everything moving on the street, and we did not have an opportunity even to move outside the cave except during the night period and for necessary things.

Things did not stop on this level but there were many other people who came to us from Jerusalem and from Abu Dis itself, and we started to hear about the Israeli army reaching Azariyeh and all the stories from the people who came about the massacres which the Israeli army had carried out in the villages around Jerusalem.

We decided to go to Jordan. We managed to stop a bus going there, and I got on it with my children and all the women and children in the cave.

Our journey was not complete because when we arrived in Jericho, there was very heavy fighting and shooting in the city, so the driver stopped the bus and asked us to go to Jericho by foot. We had to walk till we arrived at the mosque in Jericho. When we got there we found hundreds of people inside that mosque, and there were many people from Abu Dis who did not have the opportunity to leave to Jordan.

In the mosque, there was a huge problem for the people, which was how to provide their food, their water and the blankets, because the shooting outside was very heavy and nobody could go out. On that day, my children did not have any food, so I decided to go outside to try to bring them something to eat, but some of the men in the mosque refused to allow me to go out and leave my children, and they volunteered to go out, although for them it was very dangerous and they could be killed or injured. But they went out and they brought food and water for everybody, and it was enough just for one day.

On the second day, in the middle of the day, I went out of the mosque and I managed to reach one of the markets in the middle of Jericho where I found sacks of potatoes and brought them back to the mosque.

While I was in the mosque, I met Rizq Dawood Abu Hilal who was trying to go to Jordan with his family. That man used to go outside the mosque and to go near the river to find the routes that could be safe for him and for his family. But all the time he returned with very terrible stories about Israelis killing people and burying them with bulldozers.

On the morning of Friday, 10th June, a young man came to the mosque and said that there was heavy shooting towards a group of people, and Rizq Abu Hilal was with them. His sister, who was staying with us at the same mosque, went directly to that place, and she found her brother Rizq lying on the ground, and she did not manage even to recognise him, except from his clothes and because he had lost one of his fingers when he was a child. Then his brothers brought his body to the mosque before the Israeli bulldozers could bury him. After that they took him to Abu Dis and they buried him in Abu Dis.

At that time, Haj Othman, my husband, was in Abu Dis. He did not leave Abu Dis during the war. He spent all his time watching what was happening on the ground in the village. He also used to go in the night to his house, to check and to be sure that everything was safe, till he heard that there was a bus that took Abu Dis people to Jordan, and the bus had been hit by a bomb and there were many people killed and injured. That was on the fourth day of the war. So he went directly to Jericho and he did not find any transport, so he had to go by foot. On his way to Jericho, Haj Othman was thinking what a disaster it would be if he lost all of us on that bus.

On the next day I set off back to Abu Dis. I took a donkey and I put my children on it, and we arrived late that night to find that there was a curfew in Abu Dis and the villages around, and I saw the disaster which had happened to the houses and the trees and the streets in the village during the war.

This photo shows Ali Sabbah, one of the young men Naimeh Qureia mentions helping people to bring food for people in the Jericho mosque. After the 1967 war, he was in Jordan. He used to manage to come occasionally to Abu Dis, crossing the borders illegally at night, to visit his family but he was killed in 1969 by Israeli planes in Jordan. This is the only photograph his family have of him

Saleem Qureia

Saleem Qureia used to live in this old part of Abu Dis during 1967

I was 20 years old at the time of the war. I went to Jordan before the war to make cheese, with my wife and little daughter. (People from Abu Dis go to Jordan to the Bedouin there, they take milk and they make cheese and they sell it in Palestine and Amman)

I was in Madaba and I heard about the war from many stories that came to Jordan brought by the refugees talking about the massacres and the killings by the Israelis. So I rented a house and stayed there, along with my brothers who came there during the war. And each day I used to go to the bridge over the Jordan, waiting to see if my mother would arrive from Abu Dis.

Nearly all the Abu Dis people who went to Jordan at that period were in a school in Madaba. One day when I was waiting on the bridge, after a month from the beginning of the war, my mother came to Jordan, looking for me and my brothers. When she arrived, she asked me to return, because everything was now calm in Abu Dis, and she spent just one night with us before she returned back to Palestine by the bridge.

After what my mother told me, I decided to go back. Together with my sister and my uncle and my family of course, I went to the school in Madaba and tried to persuade Abu Dis people to return with me. I told them to meet him near a restaurant called al-Salaam Restaurant in Madaba, and I arranged for a truck to come and take all of us to al-Souneh.

When we arrived on the east side of the river, we waited together with nearly forty families from Abu Dis wanting to cross the river. We waited till the dark near al-Mukabar to cross. I helped many people to cross the river. We chose an area where the water was lower and people could walk in the water.

But when the first group crossed the water, four Israeli jeeps arrived and they started to shoot at the east side of the river. Because of that I took my family and we hid. We heard women and children screaming and crying in the river.

In the area where we were crossing, the river was 25 metres wide. We waited till the military vehicles moved away. There were people from the Ayyad family, Eriqat family, Bahar family, Lafee family – They also used to have a guide to take them through the bushes on a safe road to reach Jericho. But after the guide took 5 Jordanian dinars from each of us, he escaped and left us alone on the west bank of the river, and we didn't know which way to go.

At that time I found I had lost my bag with my money and my wife's clothes, and her gold. I had to go back – I returned through the river to find the bag, and I found it. But I took the wrong way back through the river and I found myself in part of the river that was more than a metre and a half high. That is what the Jordan river is like, in a metre of the river you find bits that are shallow and then bits that are very deep. Because I can't swim, I started to shout and a man called Ahmed Lafee pulled me out of the water. We had a long discussion with each other, hoping that one of us could lead the group through the bushes and take us safely to Jericho.

A man I knew from Abu Dis claimed that he knew the road, and we followed him, lost for more than 4 hours without knowing exactly where we were. So after that we stopped him, and I took my family together with some Abu Dis people, and we entered through one orchard and the rest continued on their way, and we didn't know anything about them. I collected some fruit and water melon from the orchards for my family. I met a man from Jericho who advised me not to go directly to the city; he told me that now the Israeli soldiers had methods of identifying the people who were coming from Jordan and they could notice if your clothes were wet from the river.

So he took me and my family with him to a house nearby where he allowed us to use his bathroom and we cleaned ourselves and our clothes, and he brought us a car, whose driver turned out to be one of my friends. The driver told me not to say anything when we crossed the Israeli checkpoints – he would do the talking with the soldiers.

So when we reached the first checkpoint, on the east side of Jericho, they asked us all to go out of the car. The thing that proved our story was they did not notice that our clothes were dirty or wet, so they believed us. We also stopped at another checkpoint in al-Khan al-Ahmar, and he told them the same story.

When I reached Abu Dis, I discovered that the group that I used to be with had got caught and returned to Jordan together with Ahmed Lafee, my friend.

Of course when we arrived in Abu Dis it was curfew but we managed to reach our house because it was in the old area of Abu Dis. I realised that many of my neighbours were not in their houses; they had not returned.

55

Mohammed Mousa Jaffal

Old Abu Dis with newer buildings beyond

I was ten years old when the war started. The thing I remember most strongly was that when the war started, together with my family, I joined the Jaffal family in one cave. We were about 64 people in the same cave. After one night, we went outside to al-Mrussruss area, together, and then we went direct to Jericho and spent three days in Jericho Mosque. I remember that after three days, we decided to go to Jordan, so we went on a big truck. While we were on our way to the bridge, an Israeli aeroplane dropped a bomb near the truck. My brother Ahmed was injured on his head and his hand together with two others, a man called Atiyeh Tarteer from the truck and Salemeh Jaffal. So we stopped in a small café and the people there tried to look after the injured people. After that, we continued to Jordan.

What I remember most was the very bad treatment we had from the time we arrived in Jordan. We went directly to Ma'in and we spent between three and four days there in two small rooms – we were 64 people – and I remember that we did not have food for two whole days – before we managed to have our first meal, which was bread and rice. After that, my father decided that we should leave the group and go alone to Madaba.

We spent two months in Madaba, before we decided to return to Abu Dis. When we returned, of course it was in the night and with the help of the people around who used to help people to cross the river – my father paid them money and they helped us and we crossed that night. We spent two days in Aqabat Jabal refugee camp before we returned back to Abu Dis. When we arrived in Abu Dis, after one night, the Israeli army came to our house, and they arrested my father together with two other men from our family, accusing them of coming back illegally from Jordan.

My father spent two days in investigation, and he had just one story which is that he was outside Abu Dis because it is the harvest season and he was collecting his crops, and he was not outside the West Bank.

I remember also that after nearly a month of the war, people started to discover that there were dead bodies of Jordanian soldiers in the caves around Abu Dis, and they started to collect the bodies and bury them in Abu Dis cemetery.

I have also a story about Mahmoud Jaffal. I remember that Mahmoud joined us in Jordan. He came with us in the truck that was supposed to take us to Palestine. Before the truck moved, Mahmoud's brother Saleem came to the truck and asked Mahmoud to go down and to wait for his father, and instead of Mahmoud, Saleem joined us going to Abu Dis. So Saleem lived and Mahmoud was killed.

59

Mousa Ismail Jaffal

Mousa was about 17 when the war started.

Mousa Dawood Jaffal (another member of the same family from Abu Dis) near the cave in old Abu Dis where his sister Rabeha (and 14 whole families) hid during the war. Later she went to Jordan – and did not return. Because Rabeha owned the land and the cave, people still call it Rabeha's Cave

In May 1967, Russia told Syria that Israel was preparing to have a war against Syria and Egypt. At that time all the Arab countries started to talk about liberating 1948 Palestine, and Abdul Nasser who was the leader of the Arab countries in that period started to talk about winning the war and liberating Palestine. He gave us all hope that our homeland would be free and we would have our own state.

Egypt asked all the international forces in the Sinai desert to leave their places and camps in Sinai and also the Egyptians closed Madeeq Teeran which is the place which connects Israel with the outside through the Mediterranean and Suez Canal. But also Egypt announced that they would not start the war until Israel started it.

In the morning of 5th June, the Israeli aeroplanes started their attacks on Egypt. There was a military announcement from the Egyptians on Sowt al-Arab Radio, saying that the Egyptian air defence had managed to destroy 21 Israeli planes. After that, officially Syria and Jordan announced that they would enter the war. It was clear in that period that the West Bank was under Jordanian control, so the West Bank was the field of the battles between the Israelis and the Jordanian army.

At 10 o'clock in the morning, clashes started between Israel and Jordan. At 10.30, the Jordanian radio announced that they had managed to reach Jabal al-Mukabar which used to be under Israeli control. At that period, I was still young, and I was very excited and I wanted to help, so I went out to see what was happening in al-Mukabar.

When I arrived at the place where Cliff Hotel is now, I met with a Jordanian officer who used to give orders for the Jordanian tanks to hit the Israeli locations in West Jerusalem. He asked me if I could take some ammunition to the Jordanian army in Jabal al-Mukabar, through al-Sawahreh Valley, because there would be a possible attack in the night on an Israeli settlement called Tel Beyut. I did so together with some friends from Abu Dis, and after we went down to the valley there was heavy shooting from Israeli tanks towards us, so we threw away the ammunition and ran away back to Abu Dis.

On the 5th June in the afternoon, there was an attack in the Israeli aeroplanes on a Jordanian camp in al-Khan al-Ahmar. There was an Israeli aeroplane destroyed in that location. We saw the pilot with our own eyes in his parachute and he landed on an area called al-Shamees, which is the same place now called Maale Adumim. He made a fire in that place and three planes came – one of them was a helicopter – and it managed to take him back to Israel.

All of these things happened in one day, but in the second day, early in the morning, the Israel air force also returned back to shoot at al-Khan al-Ahmar. There was a Jordanian soldier killed in a place called Abu al-Masakeen, west of Abu Dis, and the people of Abu Dis brought him and buried him here in Abu Dis. In the afternoon, the Israeli tanks started to shoot heavily in the area of al-Tour, Mount of Olives, specially around Augusta Victoria. By that day, we all believed that the Arab armies were beaten in this war, and in the evening, the people started to arrive in Abu Dis from different places in East Jerusalem. They were escaping from death, and they told us that the Israelis had already entered Jerusalem, and they were on their way to come to us in Abu Dis.

Even though we did not lose hope and we decided to stay in Abu Dis, we asked the people who arrived from Jerusalem to stay with us in the caves in and around Abu Dis.

Early next morning, about 4 o'clock, some of the Abu Dis people from different families gathered in the old Salah al-Din mosque. They had a meeting to ask about what they wanted to do, specially when they heard that the Jordanian army had started to withdraw from the village (near al-Mrussuss)

They decided that everybody must go out to the area which is east of Abu Dis to be safe and to stay in the caves there. So my family went together to a place called Abu al-Sawan, which is 3 km away from Abu Dis.

In the afternoon, the Israeli forces came to Azariyeh, and they announced by loud speaker that if anybody wanted to go to Jericho, the road was safe and open. And if anybody wanted to stay in his house, he had to raise a white flag. But because of what they had heard of massacres in 1948, the people did not believe this, and they decided to cross the Jordanian river.

As for us, on the 7th June, we joined a truck with a driver from Hebron. We were 70 people in the same truck. When we arrived in Jericho, near Aqabat Jabar camp, there was an attack by an Israeli aeroplane on the camp, and two of the people on our truck were injured, one of them called Ahmed Mousa Jaffal, and the second one was Salameh Mohammed Jaffal. But the driver did not stop, and he kept moving till we reached the river.

It was nearly seven in the evening. There were attacks from Israeli aeroplanes during the night. Because of that, the people left the vehicles. In one of the attacks, Atta Sari Eriqat was killed, and also Riziq Dawood Abu Hilal and Ismail Albow were killed in the attacks. After that attack ended, we continued our journey on foot to Amman.

We arrived in Amman at nearly 3 o'clock the next morning, and the people started directly to search for their relatives. Many people did not know exactly what had happened to their brothers or their sons. There was no news about what was happening now on the West Bank.

My family decided to stay in Jordan, but still there were many people who decided to return to their homeland by crossing the river. For us this journey lasted till 1996, when we returned to Abu Dis.

63

Sami Shehadeh Awad

I was 14 years old at the time of the June war. I heard about the war on the 5th June from the people around me – my father and the other people in my family. There were seven people in his family. My father took them all to a cave near our house. There were thirty people in that cave.

We spent two nights there, until people from al-Thowri and al-Mukabar (neighbourhoods in Jerusalem, near the Old City) came to the cave, talking about the massacres that the Israeli people had committed in their neighbourhoods, so then we decided to escape and to go to Jordan.

All the thirty people went out, walking, till we reached an area called Abu al-Sawan, and we spent two nights in a cave there. From there we heard that the Israeli army had entered Jericho and controlled the borders with Jordan. So we decided to go on to Jericho. We went to Jericho by foot, also.

While we were walking, we saw the dead body of an Israeli soldier, and an Israeli aeroplane had fallen down and was on fire.

We spent a week in Jericho inside the orchards near Wad al-Kelt – they didn't go inside the town.

When we returned back to Abu Dis, it was curfew, and we found Jordanian vehicles and tanks on our own land. They were broken and on fire. And all the way back to Abu Dis from Jericho, we saw many Jordanian vehicles on both sides of the road.

Abdullah Lafee Khilaf

Abdullah was about 12 at the time of the war.

It wasn't really a six day war; it was a six-hour war. I consider it as a game, not a real war.

At about 11 o'clock in the morning on the 5th June, the war started. On that day, the weather was good, and we were on our way to collect chickpeas from our land which is near our house, and we heard on the radio that the war had started with three Arab countries, Jordan, Syria, Egypt. Before the war, Jordanian army reinforcements had come to Abu Dis and Jerusalem and Jabal al-Mukabar, which used to be called the ceasefire line – the border with Israel. At that period, there was the Jordanian army were on Wad al-Jheer near Abu Dis Secondary School, and we used to see them shooting fire to our west, to Jerusalem, and there were some Jordanian soldiers placed on the Wall of al- Aqsa Mosque, and they did well during the war.

So then, the war started, and there was shooting between the Israelis and the Arab countries. We listened to Sowt al-Arab from Cairo, and there was Ahmed Said, who used to read the news. He was a big liar, and he used to threaten the Jews that the Arab countries would throw them to the sea and the fish would eat them. Because of this, together with the other Arab radio stations, which also used to tell these lies, we thought there was a positive atmosphere and we thought we would win this war with Israel and we get back the dignity of our nation which we had lost in 1948. We used to see aeroplanes in the sky and we thought they were Iraqi aeroplanes, but it wasn't long before we discovered that they weren't Iraqi – they were Israeli aeroplanes.

In the 1967 war, there were many young men from Abu Dis who volunteered to deliver ammunition to the Jordanian army and to the front lines of the war, specially to Jabal al-Mukabar area. There were some Jordanian soldiers at the border area and they occupied a building that used to belong to the United Nations force. But after several hours, the Israeli aeroplanes and the Israeli gunfire shot and killed them because they did not receive any ammunition or any help from the Jordanian army.

When we started to hear the news about the Israeli army reaching Abu Dis, I went with my family to a cave near our house. After three hours we moved outside Abu Dis to another cave.

We were still on the first day of the war. In the night, many people who came from Jerusalem and Silwan, and they said that the Israeli army were making massacres and they were killing men and children and raping women, like what happened in the Deir Yassin massacre.

There was an atmosphere of terror inside the cave, and my father decided that we must move to al-Aqabeh area, which was an area east of Abu Dis, near the Dead Sea. We used to see the Israeli aeroplanes just watching people going to our east, so after that we decided to go to an area called Abu al-Sawan. That area is nearly 10 km away from Abu Dis. There we stayed for two days, and during that period, we saw hundreds of people going to Jordan.

On the third day of the war, there was a bus driver, his name is Atta Eriqat who came with his bus to Abu Dis and took people from Abu Dis to Jericho; and he passed along a very bad road, not the main road, because he wanted to avoid the aeroplanes. But the bus stopped because an aeroplane dropped a bomb on it, so the people got out and went on foot to Jericho. I heard that the driver of the bus was killed by that bomb.

On the fourth day, we received news that the Israelis had entered Abu Dis, and we found out that all the stories about killing men and raping women were not true. We decided to return back to Abu Dis.

When we arrived in Abu Dis, it was very quiet. I left the house and went to our west to find some Israeli soldiers near to one of the shops in Abu Dis. They were buying some food from the shop. When I reached Kubsah I saw a Jordanian tank there on the street, and I saw many olive trees still on fire. I believe that the Israeli military at that time used some special bombs called napalm. When I returned back to my house, I found that there were some Jordanian soldiers who took off their military clothes and asked us to give them civilian clothes to escape to Jordan. One of the soldiers told us later that after that, Jordanian authorities sent him to court because he lost his army weapon and did not bring it back with him to Jordan.

I want to add here that the Jordanian army on the West Bank did not receive any support or any food from the first day of the war, and they lost all the communication with their leadership. We discovered after the war that even all the bombs that they used to shoot to the other side were fake, and I want to repeat here that that war was just like a play acted by Jordanian politicians – we are still suffering its effects till now.

Mohammed Shehadeh Mohsen

Looking over the old part of Abu Dis, past the new buildings, towards the Jordan Valley. On a clear day you can see the mountains of Jordan in the distance and sometimes the Dead Sea itself

I was 12 years old at the beginning of the war. I went with my uncle to Jordan on the 2nd June, because my family used to make cheese in Jordan, and we were in Marka which is where the airport was. On the 5th June, we watched the Israeli army bomb the Jordanian airport and destroy it. That was right at the beginning of the war.

On the second day of the war, my relatives sent me to al-Joufeh on Jabal Amman, to a school there, as a refugee, because they thought that if I was not counted with the refugees, I might never get a chance to return to Palestine.

We used to hear great speeches on the radio from King Hussein, asking people to stay on their lands, to support the Jordanian army and to resist Israel. At that time, we used to receive blankets and food from the people in Amman because we were refugees. I spent two months there in the school, together with hundreds of people. After the ceasefire and after waiting two months to return back, I lost hope and I returned to my uncle's house, and there I spent another two months before my uncle decided to find a way to return me to the West Bank.

I went with my uncle to al-Shouneh and there we spent five hours till it was dark, and we walked to al-Makhada in the night together with seven other people. When we reached the river, that was me and my uncle, we were the first people to cross the river. While we were in the middle of the water, with my uncle carrying me, there was heavy gunfire against us and against the east side of the river. After fifteen minutes in the water, we managed to reach the west side of the river and we hid inside the bushes. We didn't know exactly what had happened to the other people who were travelling with us.

While we were inside the bushes, we saw bones and bodies of human beings, and it was the first time I had ever seen wild animals eating the flesh of human beings.

We waited inside the bushes in one of the vegetable gardens till 4 o'clock in the afternoon to be sure that there were no Israelis around. After that, we managed to reach Jericho to spend that night in Jericho. There in Jericho, it was the first time I saw Israeli soldiers. I thought they were just like Americans – with white skins, and tall, just like American soldiers.

That journey from Jordan to Abu Dis took three days altogether. Those were the most difficult days in my whole life, specially when I saw the animals eating the bodies of Jordanian soldiers and civilians. And this was after four months from the beginning of the war.

While I was in Jordan, during the war, my family went out from Abu Dis for three days and then they returned back to Abu Dis.

I also remember the propaganda that used to reach us in Jordan, about the massacres that were supposed to be happening in the West Bank, which made us very afraid to return back. When I arrived in Abu Dis, I saw the new Israeli military camp, in an old hotel in Abu Dis called Cleopatra Hotel.

Hajeh Im Mohammed

Hajeh Im Mohammed was in her mid-twenties at the time of the war.

These big keys have become the symbol of Palestinian refugees. This one is the key to an old house in Abu Dis

We were living in Jordan, in the town of al-Zarka, when we heard from the Arabic radio station that Israel had started a new war against the rest of Palestine, or what we used to call the West Bank of the Jordan River.

We were very shocked about it and we started to wonder and to listen to the news – was it really a new war? We started to pray to God that the Arab countries would win this war and we would return back to our homeland.

Hours passed like years while we were waiting for news. We were very concerned about our families and our relatives in Abu Dis. We were waiting for news to reassure us.

On the second day of the war, on the 6th June, in the middle of the day, somebody knocked on the door. When I opened it, I found it was my mother-in-law together with her son and his wife and daughter. My mother-in-law was holding her gas lamp and her clothes wrapped in a cloth bundle. She had sugar and wheat and necessary clothes for the small girl who was less than a year old.

I welcomed her and I asked her to come in, and she also met my husband and my children. We brought them food and water and we thanked God that they had managed to survive and to reach us.

They started to talk about their journey from Abu Dis to Jordan and they said that they came from Abu Dis till they reached Amman, walking, coming by foot. It was only from Amman that they rented a taxi and rode to al-Zarka.

Before they finished, another family came from Abu Dis and they knocked at our door, because we were one of the first houses at the edge of the city. So we welcomed them in the same way, but the problem was our house was just two rooms, and that was a big family with seven children and their father and mother. In fact, we were six, and my mother-in-law, her son and his family were also four, so all of us together were nineteen.

So we shared the beds and everything we had, and that night the adults spent the night talking about the horrible journey which most of them had had. The next morning which was the 7th June, the family of my husband's sister which was the mother and the father, three girls and five boys, came to our house. Of course we offered them food and water and we were very happy to see them. They came from the West Bank, from Abu Dis, and we were very happy that they were safe. The family that we had before were very embarrassed because they knew that there was no room for them to stay and they wanted to give space for my husband's sister and her family, but of course we refused to let them go, because we knew that they did not have anywhere to go.

Then we heard on the Jordanian radio that they were calling for all the refugees from Palestine to go to the schools and they gave the names of all the schools in the neighbourhoods and the villages that could put up refugees; they added that refugees would find everything they needed in these schools – water, food, a place to sleep, blankets, everything. These were given by the Jordanian authorities together with UNWRA.

The family which we hosted the previous night found this a good opportunity and they excused themselves and went to one of the schools which is in our neighbourhood. We asked them, if they did not find the school comfortable, to return to us and we could manage with each other in this crisis. So they went out to one school, along with thousands of other refugees, but they did not find any place to stay in there. After three days, my husband decided to visit them and to see how they were managing in that school, but when he got to the school, he saw a real crisis, and a view which he will never forget in his life. It was like Armageddon. The school was full of people, and also the main playground of the school. Children were crying. And there were groups of people fighting over places to sleep in.

My husband asked about our friend whose name was Abu Ali, and after nearly one hour he managed to find him. When he asked him about life there and about his family, the man started to cry. My husband tried to cheer him up, saying that this would end soon, but Abu Ali asked how he could manage not to cry with all the humiliation and pressure they were living under: they couldn't sleep, they couldn't eat. My husband asked about the announcements on the radio – they were supposed to have food and they were supposed to have places to sleep. Abu Ali said that if he had known that this would happen to his family, he would have preferred to have stayed in his house and die in Palestine:

"I destroyed my life and I destroyed my family when I decided to go out of Palestine, I wish I had stayed in my house near my olive trees and my farm – that would be a hundred times better than coming here and enduring this humiliation.

"About the life in the school, the UNWRA bring sardines in tins and give one tin to each family and one blanket for each family. They turn on the water for us just for two hours each day, and imagine how crowded it is around the one tap that we have. You have to go through a major suffering just to reach the water and get some water for your family to drink. And also don't ask about the bathrooms – there are three doors for all the people here and it is a real misery when you want to enter one of them. Nobody can handle this humiliation, and I can't stay here, I want to return to my country. I will find a way and I will try to cross the river together with my family."

After 5 days of the war, Israel closed the borders and refused to allow any Palestinian to return to his own country. After three months, Abu Ali managed to contact the people who help the refugees to return and cross the river, and he made a deal with someone to meet his family near the east side of the river, and to try to help them to cross. On that day, Abu Ali and his wife came to us in our house to say goodbye. And in our house he sat together with his children and wife and he started to talk seriously to his family and told them

"You will never find any place on this earth better than your own homeland and if you manage to return back, whether I or your mother live or die, then you should please stay in your house and never leave it again, because you saw what happened to you at that school. The human being without a homeland is like a body without a soul. You have to protect and to defend your homeland."

When he had finished, he took his family and he went to the river and while they were crossing the river, an Israeli military vehicle came. Before it reached them, Abu Ali managed to hide his children on one of the farms, but the soldiers captured Abu Ali and took him to an unknown place and he has not returned back till now.

If you are living in your home and somebody simply came to steal your home from you, what will you do? Will you leave your home to the strangers or will you fight and do everything to have your house back?

The first six days

The context

Men of the Abu Hilal family dancing at a wedding in Abu Dis before 1967

1967: the historical context

In the period before the June War, there were many inside conflicts in the Arab countries which made the Arab countries very weak during the war. We still suffer in the Arab countries from this. The Arab countries used to be in two camps: the first one, which is the national camp led by Egypt and its leader Jamal Abdul Nasser, included Syria, Iraq and Algeria, and the second camp which used to be with the West, the capitalist camp, and included Saudi Arabia, Jordan, Libya, Tunisia and Morocco.

The conflict was very strong between these camps, specially after Egypt got involved in Yemen against the Western camp, because Jamal Abdul Nasser sent his army to support the revolution, which overthrew the monarchy in Yemen. At the same time, Saudi Arabia, together with the Jordanians, sent armies to support the system in Yemen. This war continued for many years, and weakened the ability of Arab countries to unite in face of the Israeli danger.

Three years before the war, in 1964, the PLO was created in Jerusalem and was recognised by the Arab world as the only representative of the Palestinian people. Through this organisation, a number of military groups were created in Syria and in the Gaza Strip. In 1965, the Fateh movement was also created as a national resistance movement against the occupation, and they made a number of military operations against Israeli targets across the Syrian and Jordanian borders. Israel responded with serious attacks across the borders and built up their military force near those areas.

In the Gaza Strip, the Palestinian liberation army, which belonged to the PLO, started to work against the Israeli targets under the supervision of the Egyptians. The situation in the West Bank was different from the Gaza Strip because Jordan considered the West Bank a part of its kingdom and saw the Palestinians under Jordanian rule as Jordanians. Nobody there was allowed to

SALAH AYYAD,
Member of Abu Dis Town Council

create or join a political party. Further, the Jordanians did not allow the people in the West Bank to communicate with the national camp led by Egypt, and there was punishment under Jordanian law if anybody was caught listening to radio stations from these countries.

With the start of the Palestinian resistance, Israel attempted to provoke problems with Syria: Israel wanted Syria to attack them in order to take land from Syria and make it a closed area (an area without weapons), and also to have full control over Lake Tiberias. Palestinian resistance operations from Syria and the West Bank continued, and Israel launched many attacks against the Palestinians, specially on the West Bank. In al-Samouah village, near Hebron, the Israeli army destroyed the village houses and killed many of the villagers and some Jordanian soldiers who tried to help the people.

After al-Samouah, the Palestinian and Jordanian people felt that their country couldn't protect the borders with Israel, so an intifada against the Jordanian regime began in the cities of both the East and the West Banks. For several weeks, people called on the Jordanian regime to co-ordinate with the countries of the national camp, to empower the Jordanian army and to give weapons to the ordinary people to protect themselves and do their duty in defending their homeland. But instead of doing what the public wanted, the Jordanian regime started to punish the people, and many of the people who joined this intifada were killed or arrested.

At that time Egypt had a United Nations force in the Sinai desert and on the Egyptian national water at Sharm al-Sheikh. When Israel attacked the borders of Syria and Jordan, the Arab Western camp challenged Egypt's leadership of the Arab countries by accusing Jamal Abdul Nasser of hiding behind the international force. Israel now increased its threat towards Syria, and because Egypt was a leader of the Arab countries, Egypt had to take some action.

In May 1967, when the Israeli attacks reached a very high level, Jamal Abdul Nasser ordered the international force to leave Sinai. He put the Egyptian army on the borders. Within days, the Jordanian King Hussein visited Cairo and signed a mutual defence agreement with Abdul Nasser. The Egyptian government appointed a commander for the Jordanian front and King Hussein sent his army to the borders between the West Bank and Israel; a similar agreement was made between the Syrians and the Egyptians.

The new Egyptian leader of the Jordanian army did not have a chance to gain proper information about the situation on the ground and the situation of the army. At this point, the Jordanian government finally allowed Ahmed al-Shoukiry, leader of the PLO, to visit Jerusalem. But this was after a long period in which he had been prevented from coming there, and he did not have time to help his people to prepare for the war.

Jordanian army reinforcements were sent to the borders in the West Bank in a hurry, and the Jordanian government did not prepare the people for a war; they did not arm them or even find safe places for them to stay during the war. They did not train them for self-defence or public defence. The streets and different bridges were not secure. People started to organise themselves, and to clean their own caves and to save some food, because they felt that a war would come any time. Also they were sure that the Arab armies would do the job themselves, and would fight without any need for the people to help. So the war started in a very bad way, with a weak relation between the people and the government, and no ability to create political parties or national movements which could lead the people or support the army and the country during the war. This is why the Palestinians found themselves in a few days under Israeli occupation.

Anyway, the war started on the morning of 5th June, and there was no fighting on the Jordanian front till 10 o'clock in the morning. By that time, the Israeli aeroplanes had destroyed the Egyptian airports and aeroplanes and the Israeli army had reached the Suez Canal with the cover of their air force which was now controlling the sky on nearly all the fronts. So at 10 o'clock the Israeli aeroplanes started to attack the Jordanian army, and some Iraqi units came to help the Jordanian army in the West Bank.

Within two days and with the help of napalm bombs, which were used in a very wide way against the military camps and units in the West Bank and East Jordan, all the communications, roads and bridges between the different units had been cut, and it was impossible to send any ammunitions or any food to these units. Before the war, the Jordanian army sent many units and tanks to Abu Dis and Jerusalem, but at the beginning of the war, some of these units tried to reach Jabal al-Mukabar but were forced to return back to Abu Dis after hours because of the heavy shooting from the Israeli tanks and aeroplanes specially in the area of Augusta Victoria, on the Mount of Olives, and Sheikh Jarrah and the western area of Abu Dis. Although these units survived, and managed to stay in their positions, they had no food and could not continue.

People from Abu Dis tried to help the Jordanian army by sending them ammunition and sending them food and trying to help the injured soldiers, but after two days of bombing from tanks and the air, and with some attacks from the Israeli soldiers on the ground, many Jordanian soldiers were killed. There is a special place in Jerusalem now with the names of all the Jordanian soldiers who were killed defending the holy city of Jerusalem.

On the third day of the war, and after instructions from the Jordanian commander for the Jordanian army to withdraw to the east, we started to notice the collapse and chaos in the whole West Bank, and the Jordanian soldiers started to run away in a disorganised way. The Israelis could now easily control all the places that the Jordanians withdrew from. The Israeli army started to enter the different cities and villages in the West Bank without any resistance. This sort of chaos usually happens when a defence army withdraws and when there is not enough awareness from the people and they are not ready for their army to be defeated.

There was a big emigration of people because they were very afraid of the Israeli army. People started to leave their houses, specially the houses which were near the borders and to go east. And while they were travelling, when they entered any Palestinian village on their way to Jordan, and these stories were an exaggeration. Some of them started to talk about the Israelis massacring young people in the villages and neighbourhoods which fell under the Israeli control. This had happened in 1948 in places such as Deir Yassin and Jaffa, and there had been other massacres by the Israelis after that. So as the memories of the events in 1948 were still there in the minds of that generation, people believed what they heard and they started to run away from the West Bank, going east.

Waves of people started to go to the Jordanian river. Some of them used their animals to carry the old people and the children because they did not find any transport. The number of people increased in each village that they passed through. Some of them crossed the river and continued to Jordan. Some of them went out of their villages and stayed in the caves around the villages and then returned back home; while others reached the Jordanian borders near the river, but they found that the Israeli army had reached the river before them, because Israeli military units had come along the Dead Sea from the south, some of them came through Beesan in the north, and so they controlled all the east borders with Jordan. Also in this way, they managed to occupy all the West Bank including East Jerusalem in a very short time.

During the emigration, there were many people who got killed and injured because the Israeli aeroplanes used to drop bombs everywhere specially on the roads, and so much chaos that many people left their injured people, old people and children on the streets as they ran to survive. The results were that nearly 700,000 Palestinians left their homeland to go to Jordan. Many of them of course started to think about returning home, after days and weeks. The Israeli army did not yet control all the borders with Jordan so many people managed to return by crossing the river, specially at night, but you can say thousands of them paid with their lives and died while they were crossing the river.

There were many whole families killed by the Israeli snipers while they were trying to cross the river, specially at night because the Israeli soldiers used to shoot anything that moved and shoot at the sides of the river while the Israeli bulldozers used to bury the bodies of hundreds of people in the daylight.

People went on trying to cross the river for about three months. The Israeli army at that period increased their procedures on the border, and took statistics of people in Gaza and the West Bank. The Palestinian military organisations took positions on the east side of the river, and they started to go for military operations against the Israelis inside the occupied territories. So after three months, it was very dangerous for the people to cross.

After the Jordanian army left the West Bank, Israelis entered Jerusalem and some places in the north around Jenin, and the Jordanian Valley area. But there were many small villages which the Israeli army did not even enter directly after the ceasefire. Later they entered the villages one by one with a huge force, and they started to make searches of the houses, caves etc, everywhere in the villages, looking for the ammunition that the Jordanian army had left behind.

At the beginning of the war, many houses in Abu Dis were destroyed by the Israeli air force. Many Jordanian soldiers and many civilians were killed and wounded, and people just buried them in a hurry together in the special open grave (fuzqarah), where people used to bury children who had died.

During the war, the Israelis destroyed the electricity net and the water net which used to supply the west side of Abu Dis, the side which belonged to Jerusalem Municipality. Although the Israeli army took all the heavy weapons which were left behind by the Jordanian army, they left the ammunition around the houses and in the valleys in Abu Dis, which caused huge harm, especially when some children played with it. One child was killed and many were wounded.

When the Israeli soldiers entered Abu Dis and while they were searching in the houses, they removed many valuable things from inside the houses, even some furniture. That was not a personal behaviour, it was a programme organised by their leadership. They specially took electrical items, like refrigerators, televisions, radios, and they used to put them inside a huge military pick-up, under the supervision of their commanders. Many of the Palestinian people watched the Israeli army while they were stealing from their houses and it seemed that the officers from the Israeli army took things for their own private use. This shows that when Moshe Dayan (Defence Minister of Israel at that time) fired some of the officers in the Israeli army for stealing wheat from some Arab houses, it was just for the media and was not sincere.

People were humiliated in the streets in the Palestinian cities and villages and there were Israeli military vehicles in the main streets announcing curfew and shooting fire in the air to terrify the Palestinians. All this happened as the wild Israeli army entered the West Bank, and this was the beginning of the long Occupation for us.

85

This part of the Jaffal family: Dawood Mohammed Jaffal, his son Mahmoud, daughter Rabeha and her sons. They all disappeared when they were crossing the River Jordan to return to Abu Dis

Life in Abu Dis before and after 1967

SALEH ABU HILAL
with
ABDUL WAHAB SABBAH

The war started in the first days of the school summer holiday. At that period, before the war, the schools in Jerusalem and Abu Dis were very crowded. The classrooms used to include 40 boys in each class. What happened after the war, in September, was that each teacher received a letter from the Israeli authority asking him to return back to his work. But the Jordanian Ministry of Education made an announcement on the radio that the teachers should not return back because the schools were under Occupation, and so some of the teachers refused to return, and because of that, the schools did not work till November.

In November, the Israeli authorities started to send the teachers from the West Bank out of Jerusalem schools. I was moved by the Israeli authorities from al-Essawiyeh School in Jerusalem to teach in Abu Dis Boys' School. I noticed that out of six hundred students who had been in Abu Dis Boys' School, there were now only two hundred boys.

After 1967, the Israeli authorities started to send Israeli employees to the school as school inspectors. They spoke the Arabic language well. They used to search the libraries and the books in the schools, and they took away all the books which mentioned the name Palestine, or the borders of Palestine, or anything that talked about Palestine as a state. They started to change the curriculum and also some of the students left school, even at the primary age. Before the Occupation, nobody was allowed to be out of school at that age, but after Israel there was no control and some of the children found work inside Israel and went there instead of to school. There was nothing to stop Palestinian children working on building sites, and this was cheap labour for Israel.

Directly after the Occupation, Israel announced that most of the land right outside Abu Dis on the east side was now military closed zones. After 1978, this land began to be taken for Israeli settlements like Maale Adumim, Mushur Adumim and

Kedar. This was a big problem for people dependent on agriculture, either people who grew crops in that area or people who used that land for grazing. Abu Dis land used to be 16 square kilometres, but after the Occupation, it was reduced to 4 square kilometres.

From the point of view of work, in Abu Dis, during the Jordanian period, many people in Abu Dis had work in the Jordanian army and in the Gulf States, in building work in East Jerusalem and also agriculture in Abu Dis. After the war, people lost the opportunity to travel outside in a free way – it was not easy to go to the Gulf. Most of the workers in the Jordanian army had left to Jordan, specially the soldiers, who were very afraid of the Israeli punishment and many of them have not returned. Also people started to leave the land and agriculture and to work in Israel because it gave more money quickly and because they could not use their land. It was part of Israeli policy too to make people leave their lands.

During the Jordanian rule, seventy per cent of people depended completely on wells, and there was no mains water supply in Abu Dis right up till 1970. In the days before the war, there was an announcement by the Jordanian government asking people to pay money to an electrical company who would supply electricity to the whole of Abu Dis. Only ten per cent of Abu Dis people had electricity up till then. But the war started and there was not the chance for most people to get electricity supplies.

About health during the Jordanian period – there were no formal health services in Abu Dis, just one nurse who used to give people advice. People could get advice from people who knew traditional medicine, or use traditional midwives, or else they went to a hospital in Jerusalem called al-Hospees.

During Jordanian rule, people used to deal with the government through the offices in Jerusalem – for things like birth certificates or permission to build, etc. After the Occupation, they made a new system. They appointed a mukhtar in each village to be the link between the people and the Occupation authority, and nobody was allowed to communicate directly to the authority except via the mukhtar. (Note this was a different system from the traditional one when of each family elected their own mukhtar as clan leader)

Before the war, the population of Abu Dis was 6000, some of whom were out working. After the war, at least half the people who were actually living in Abu Dis, had gone. People who had been preparing to return to Abu Dis also stayed outside, so after Abu Dis, there were only 3000 left, because of the Occupation.

89

90

The first six days

Maps

Israel/Palestine after the 1967 war

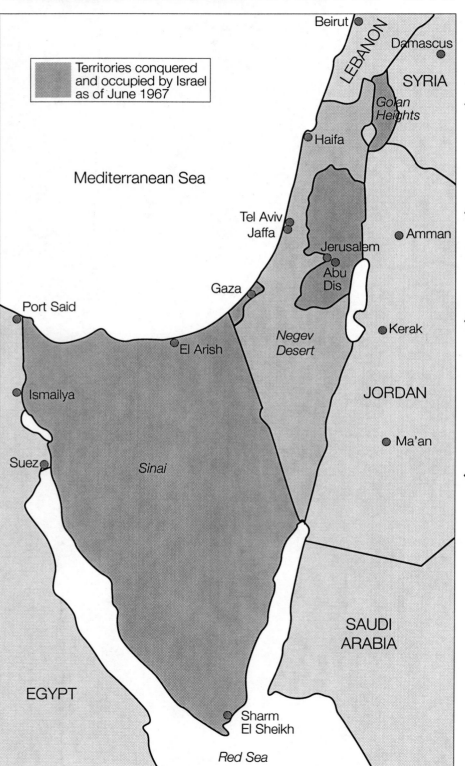

Abu Dis, before and after 1967

A view of Camden's main street

The first six days

Camden memories

Three memories of 1967 from Camden

One

Really I can't remember, I get so muddled up – Was it Suez? There were so many wars.

Two

I was at primary school in 1967, but I do remember it. At that point my teacher made us do projects, which seemed to consist of cutting things out and sticking them in a book, and for some reason I decided to cut out bits about the war in the Middle East and stick them in a book. I remember what I thought, too… I was walking down the road with a group of students at school, and someone said "Whose side are you on?" – a bit like which football team you support.

One of the boys said "Definitely not the Yids" and that was a very unpopular position – I wonder now from his surname if his family was of Arabic origin – there was no one else there who thought like that. Immediately he was on his own and everyone on the other side.

I thought Israel was a small brave clean country and I was very pleased they won so simply.

Three

I didn't have the least understanding of it – I didn't have the time or inclination to read newspapers about it – I depended on the BBC – I didn't know the background of it. There had been wars before that, hadn't there, that went the other way I think…

I remember in 1948 when Israel started, I was happy – I knew about the pogroms there had been against Jews in Europe and it seemed a good thing they had a country of their own..

I don't think I really understood anything about it for years, but it seems to me that nowadays that a lot of people are beginning to realise, they see that Israel is the bully boy of that region…

Ruth Tenne

Now a member of Camden Abu Dis Friendship Association (CADFA), Ruth was born on a kibbutz in Israel and came to London in 1969. In her interview, she included an account of what happened to her after 1967, to explain how she has changed her view dramatically since that time.

Ruth shows us evidence of the long journey she has travelled from a Zionist heritage to taking a stand against Israel's wrong-doing. She holds a Jewish National Fund certificate for planting a tree in her name, awarded to her as a school prize; beneath it is a placard she has carried in rallies protesting against Israel's policies

I was studying at the time for my second degree in Haifa, and then we heard that there were some skirmishes on both the Syrian borders, the Golan Heights (which wasn't ours) and in Sinai, and we were aware that something was going on. And we were aware that people were getting enlisted to the reserves and I remember I spoke to my friend and we were very worried. We had the feeling that we were all encircled by the Egyptian and also the Syrian army and we were terrified. We knew that they were very much against Israel, of course. The Egyptians at the time were the worst enemy, we didn't think of the Palestinians at all, and Jordan wasn't at the time involved, they joined in later on.

Now I remember that my brother was studying in Jerusalem and he was a parachutist. I got a lift with a friend and went to see him because I was very worried about what would happen to him. When I came to Jerusalem he had gone, and I knew if he was already enlisted that meant that Israel was preparing for a war.

I went back to Haifa again to get on with my studies, and then in the middle of the night I got a summons for the Reserve Army. I didn't actually think that they would call me up – normally when you are of an age over twenty-something they don't call you up – but I wasn't married and there is a law that if you are unmarried, they are still entitled to call you up. I had to go to some place in the morning, it was still in Haifa, just outside Haifa, and I went there in the morning, and we got some instruction and we were part of what you call the Civil Defence. We didn't have to do much, but in the evening we had to go to the neighbourhoods and tell people not to put the light on, or in the back they had to put the shutters down – so we went from one house to another just chatting to people, saying "It's a blackout."

That was, I believe, two or three days before… I believe that I didn't go on duty for more than two nights and I went with some other women. There were some men as well there, but basically women – the men went to the front. We went back to the camp in Haifa, a special army camp, where we stayed the night.

In the morning, the 5th June, the Israeli airforce launched a strike on the Egyptian air force and they crushed them all in one go, and I remember one of the commanders saying, "Now you can go home, the war is over, we are the winners." And what did we have after that? Maybe we had some parties – but we had won. I went back to my studies. Most of my colleagues were at the front but I was away only two days. My brother was still on the front.

And then at that time, Jordan joined in… but still at that time, Egypt was the worst enemy. We were glued to the radio all the time to hear the news - the television wasn't in existence at that time. Then we heard that our airforce had hit the Egyptian troops in the Sinai desert and on the Golan Heights as well. I wasn't sure if my brother was on the Golan Heights or in Jerusalem; we hadn't heard from him for quite a long time. I was extremely worried about him.

If you asked me what happened then, I don't think that the Palestinian question ever crossed my mind. I remember that the main agenda was whether we had to return the Sinai desert to the Egyptians. One of my lecturers was quite a peaceful person and she said we had to give the land back. I didn't understand that: many people in my brother's unit had been killed, I thought we had sacrificed a lot of people, why should we return Sinai? That was my thinking at the time.

The Palestinian question wasn't really a great issue at the time. I remember that at one time we went on a visit to Jericho. But I can't remember that I ever saw a Palestinian. We went along the roads; we didn't see the refugee camps as far as I remember, we just saw the Jordan Valley. It didn't actually cross my mind at all - what we were concerned about was the Egyptian enemy. At the time, there was no question of settlements. Until about ten years after 1967 there were very few settlements – only about 5,000 people in the first ten years.

After 1967

I left Israel at the end of 1969 and then I had some friends who were peace campaigners. We had a lot of debate and we started to realise that our story, the Israeli story, was not the full story or the real story. I started to read in English, see the newspapers and watch the news on television. In Israel you get only the Israeli story. Even when I came here, it took me some time to get to know the other side, to read about it and to adopt a different sort of view.

When I went to Israel in 1972, that was my only visit. I debated the issue of Palestine and I told my friends that Israel was wrong, especially the way that they killed the Palestinians. I believed at the time that we had to withdraw from the occupied territories – then it was just a question of military withdrawal, as there were not that many settlements. Likud came into power in the 70s and then the settlement movement really took off.

1982 was really a turning point for me – the invasion of Lebanon – I just couldn't put up with it – I couldn't see how Israel had the right to invade another country. I knew that the Golan Heights was still in the hands of the Israeli Occupation and there were clashes on the border, but I couldn't understand why Israel was invading Lebanon. The name of the Israeli operation was very bad and misleading, "Peace for Galilee." From then on I started to be more active.

Still I wasn't fully aware. But reading more and more about the settlement policy and about all the newcomers, who used the Right of Return Law to come from America and all over Europe to settle in Israel and take the land of the Palestinians, that was inconceivable to me … And then in 87, the first intifada – you remember the picture that went around the world of Israeli soldiers breaking bones of Palestinians … It was just a resistance by young Palestinians and I couldn't understand how Israel could shoot these young people…

I heard of Jews for Justice for Palestinians about 3 or 4 years ago and thought we should do something to face up to the Israeli propaganda. I thought it was my duty to write to the press as an Israeli who is prepared to stand up to her own country's policies. I thought actually this would have a great impact. Then of course I heard about CADFA.

The invasion of Lebanon broke my heart. I think I felt cheated to some extent; my parents were staunch Zionists, they believed in social order, a society that wouldn't discriminate against sex or race and would live in harmony with its Palestinian and Arab neighbours. When I was in the kibbutz, I thought that was what we were doing… I did see all these Arab villages razed to the ground, but it still didn't hit me - I followed what my parents said, that we had a right to the land, and we had been there before…

Now I feel cheated by my parents – Why did they never ever discuss with me the question of the Palestinians?

Camden Abu Dis Friendship Association

CADFA works in Camden to promote awareness about the human rights situation in Abu Dis and Palestine. Our objects are below.

As part of this work we are building friendship links between individuals and organisations in Camden and Abu Dis and supporting a number of projects in Abu Dis. Information about the Camden links groups and the projects they are supporting can be found on our website:
www.camdenabudis.org

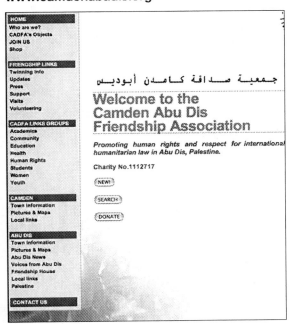

CADFA's objects

are to promote human rights (as set out in the Universal Declaration of Human Rights and subsequent United Nations conventions and declarations) and respect for international humanitarian law in the area of Abu Dis, a region of Palestine, by all or any of the following means:

- Raising awareness of human rights and humanitarian issues relevant to the Israeli-Palestinian conflict in general and to the situation of Abu Dis in particular;

- Researching and monitoring abuses of human rights and infringements of humanitarian law in Abu Dis;

- Educating the public about human rights and humanitarian law;

- Promoting public support for human rights and the observance of humanitarian law;

- Working to eliminate abuses of human rights and infringements of humanitarian law in Abu Dis;

- Working to obtain and promote redress for the victims of human rights abuses and infringements of humanitarian law in Abu Dis and their families;

- Providing support to and relieving need among the victims of human rights abuses and infringements of humanitarian law and their families, in Abu Dis.

More information from:
contact@camdenabudis.org

Printed in the United Kingdom
by Lightning Source UK Ltd.
133298UK00001B/105-172/A